D1636655

JOHN AUGUSTUS
FIRST PROBATION OFFICER

PATTERSON SMITH REPRINT SERIES IN
CRIMINOLOGY, LAW ENFORCEMENT, AND SOCIAL PROBLEMS

A listing of publications in the SERIES *will be found at rear of volume*

PUBLICATION No. 130: PATTERSON SMITH REPRINT SERIES IN CRIMINOLOGY, LAW ENFORCEMENT, AND SOCIAL PROBLEMS

JOHN AUGUSTUS

FIRST PROBATION OFFICER

John Augustus' original Report of his Labors (1852)
with an Introduction by Sheldon Glueck
and illustrations

first published 1939
by the National Probation Association;
Reprinted with a new Preface
and an Index

PATTERSON SMITH
MONTCLAIR, NEW JERSEY
1972

A Report of the Labors of John Augustus
first published 1852 by Wright & Hasty, Boston, Mass.
Reprinted 1939 with additional material as
John Augustus, First Probation Officer
by the National Probation Association
Reprinted 1972 by Patterson Smith Publishing Corporation
by special arrangement with the
National Council on Crime and Delinquency
(formerly the National Probation Association)
New material copyright © 1972 by
Patterson Smith Publishing Corporation
Montclair, New Jersey 07042

Library of Congress Cataloging in Publication Data

Augustus, John, 1785–1859.
John Augustus, first probation officer.

(Patterson Smith reprint series in criminology,
law enforcement, and social problems. Publication
no. 130)
First published in 1852 under title: A report of
the labors of John Augustus, for the last ten
years, in aid of the unfortunate . . .
Reprint of the 1939 ed. with a new introduction
and index.
1. Probation—Boston. 2. Boston—Charities.
HV9306.B7A8 1972 364.6′3′0924 [B] 79-129308
ISBN 0-87585-130-4

This book is printed on
permanent/durable paper

CONTENTS

PREFACE TO THE
NEW EDITION

JOHN AUGUSTUS published his account of the first ten years of his philanthropic work in 1852—at the request of his friends, as he modestly tells us. In 1939 the National Probation Association reissued Augustus' pamphlet in facsimile, with an introduction by Sheldon Glueck, then Professor of Criminal Law at Harvard Law School, and a foreword by Charles L. Chute, the Executive Director of the Association. The present edition retains all this material and adds an index to the Report: it is published under the auspices of the Association's successor, the National Council on Crime and Delinquency, and marks the enormous growth that the probation system has enjoyed—both in its application by the courts and in its acceptability to the public—in the last three decades.

For probation is finally coming into its own. After rising steadily from the end of the Second World War to a peak of 220,000 in 1961, the number of inmates in state prisons then began to decline: in 1967, the latest year for which complete figures are available, the state prison population was down to 175,317. In view of the increase both in the total population and in the crime rate, this is an extraordinary decrease; and it is mainly attributable to the greatly expanded use of probation, and other forms of community treatment, as an alternative to prison sentences. Like other countries, the United States is, at long last, finding that probation is the answer to prison reform.

A reason why the promise of probation was so long unfulfilled is that, in the United States, it developed as a professional service. When Glueck wrote in 1939 the nation could apparently afford fewer than 5,000 probation and parole officers; today, with adult probation laws on the statute books of all the states of the Union, there are 25,000, but it is still a rare department that is adequately staffed. Until recently only a small effort was made in the direction of establishing a volunteer corps, and in fact Glueck implied that before the Second World War this was scarcely encouraged. But it was as volunteer work that Augustus undertook probation, and now, 130 years after he set forth this approach, we are seeing it applied on a large scale. Volunteers in Probation, now a program of NCCD and many times larger than all the professional probation bodies, has stimulated volunteer service in hundreds of courts dealing with misdemeanors, courts that had previously had no probation service whatsoever.

This is therefore a fitting time to take another look at the Labors of John Augustus—of the man who set the probation system in motion, but whose example is only now coming to be followed as closely as it deserved.

MILTON G. RECTOR, *Executive Director*
National Council on Crime and Delinquency

Paramus, New Jersey
February 1972

FOREWORD TO THE
1939 EDITION

WE reproduce in this little volume the original pamphlet edition of the quaint autobiographical story, *The Labors of John Augustus*. It is of historical and human interest and is a unique contribution to the work in which he was the undoubted pioneer. The first to invent a system, which he termed probation, of selection and supervision of reformable offenders in the criminal courts, he labored in their behalf for eighteen years until his death in Boston in 1859 at the age of seventy-five. Although his service to unfortunates was purely voluntary, he became in fact the first probation officer. After him others carried on the work which led to the enactment in 1878 of the first probation law in the world, providing for a salaried officer for the Boston courts. From that beginning the authorized use of probation spread to all the courts of Massachusetts, to other New England states, and gradually to states westward and southward, to England and to other European countries.

For the following biographical notes, supplementing and confirming John Augustus' own account, we are indebted to a painstaking research of original town records and old books conducted by Mrs. Robert W. Fernald of Lexington, Massachusetts, and to Eldon R. James, librarian of the Law School of Harvard University.

John Augustus was born at Woburn, Massachusetts, in 1784. He moved to Lexington at the age of twenty-one and became a cordwainer, or shoemaker, by trade. From 1811 to 1827 he owned and occupied the famous old Jonathan Harrington house in Lexington and carried on his shoemaking establishment in the ell of that house. His business evidently prospered and he became a man of substance as shown by records that he owned a large tract of land and that in 1819 he conveyed to the trustees of the Lexington Academy between eight and nine acres of this land for the purpose of erecting the school of which he became a trustee.

In 1827 he removed to Boston and continued his bootmaking. In 1841 at the age of fifty-seven Augustus "happened to be in court one day and heard a man arraigned for drunkenness. The man could not pay his fine. John Augustus requested that the man be allowed a short probation period and be placed in his care."[1]

His first interest was in drunkards. "Their improved conduct brought a small fine instead of imprisonment and disgrace. For the first year he took only men, then unfortunate women. John Augustus, in 'all proper cases,' was always ready with bail. This annoyed the officers but he was supported by the judges and the press.

"For the first several years he spent nearly his all on bails and fines for his 'charges.' Out of two thousand for whom he became responsible only ten proved ungrateful and absconded.

"The unceasing calls upon his time destroyed his business as bootmaker. He was not discouraged by lack of funds. Later a few friends helped him. . . .

"Up to 1858 he had bailed out 1152 men and 794 women and girls. . . . In addition to those bailed he had helped 'over three thousand females who, being neglected by the world, had no sympathy or protection but what he volunteered to furnish them.'"[2]

John Augustus had his enemies as do all pioneers. They thought his methods an incentive to crime. They charged him with selfishness, insincerity and greed. They called him a mock philanthropist. To them he replied: "While it saves the county and state hundreds, and I may say thousands of dollars, it drains my pockets instead of enriching me. To

1. Lexington town records, compiled by Thomas J. Canavan and preserved in typewritten form in the Cary Library, Lexington.

2. From "Letter Concerning the Labors of Mr. John Augustus, the Well-known Philanthropist, From One Who Knew Him." Anonymous. Published for private circulation, Boston, 1858. The book was presented to the Boston Public Library by the Hon. Edward Everett, June 21, 1859.

attempt to make money by bailing poor people would prove
an impossibility. . . . The first year and the three or four
years following I worked hard at my business in my shop.
Sometimes I worked all night to make up for the time I had
spent in court. I was obliged to prepare work for my workmen and thus my duties were extremely laborious. I expended
all I earned for four years by hard labor at my trade besides
what aid I received from others. The first two years (1841-2)
I received nothing from anyone except what I earned by my
daily labor; in 1843 I received from various persons in aid
of my work, $758; in 1844-5-6 I received $1213 each year.
I then gave up business at my shop and for the last five years
my receipts have averaged yearly $1776, all of which I have
expended and have not a dollar of this sum.'' (p. 103)

It was said of this truly great character that he was possessed of undying energy. He often had as many as fifteen
of his proteges living in his house at one time. He drove about
in a one-horse shay, and in fact wore out two or three shays
in his visits to his probationers. ''He had a kind word and a
charitable act for even the vilest offender, regardless of race,
nationality or social position. . . . He never refused the pleas
of those who knocked at his door.''

This brief foreword about the life and labors of the little
known originator of a new, humane, and at the same time
scientific method of dealing with the offender is followed by
an introductory statement prepared by Sheldon Glueck, Professor of Criminal Law, Harvard University Law School, and
by the report of John Augustus himself, reproduced exactly
from the original publication. We express sincere apprecia-
tion to Professor Glueck for suggesting that the National
Probation Association reprint this record. To him and also
to Eldon R. James, librarian, Harvard Law School, go our
thanks for making available a copy of the report, copies of
the original scrolls and the photograph of John Augustus,
which are the treasured possessions of the library; to Mrs.
Robert W. Fernald for obtaining the notes and the photo-
graphs of the old home and the tomb of the pioneer.

It is our hope that this publication may contribute to an understanding of the bases upon which rest not only modern probation but social service in all its branches. May it stimulate interest and deeper understanding and so contribute to the further growth of the service in which we are engaged.

CHARLES L. CHUTE, *Executive Director*
National Probation Association

May 1939

HOME OF JOHN AUGUSTUS
1811-1828, Lexington, Massachusetts

TOMB OF JOHN AUGUSTUS
Old Cemetery, Lexington, Massachusetts

INTRODUCTION TO THE 1939 EDITION

I

EVERY profession has its geniuses, heroes, inspirers of those who come after. Medicine boasts of its Hippocrates, Vesalius, Pasteur, Reed; Law of its Mansfield, Blackstone, Marshall, Holmes. A name too little known among workers in the correctional field is that of John Augustus, the Boston maker of shoes who, in the middle of the past century, devoted much of his time, ingenuity and means to the making of decent citizens out of criminals. John Augustus is in a very real sense the father of probation.

If it be true that "the evil that men do lives after them, the good is oft interred with their bones," then, to reverse this law of ingratitude in even one instance is a public service. That is one good reason why the writer has undertaken to bring out this little known chronicle of the labors of a man who indeed deserves to be remembered by his fellowmen. But it is not the only reason.

Within the pages of John Augustus' quaint account of his stewardship of offending humanity is to be found much wisdom still untarnished by the passage of time; wisdom not only for judges and probation officers, but for social workers generally and indeed for all who believe in the essential goodness of humanity.

This account of Augustus' humane and wise ministry was published by him in Boston in 1852, at the request of his friends, "with diffidence yet with much self-gratification." It covers his activities in the Boston criminal courts during a ten year period prior to its publication. Evidently only a small number of copies was printed, and most of these appear to have gone the customary way of occasional pamphlets. The surviving copies of the original printed edition of Augustus' report are not readily accessible; hence a reprint ought to be of value to probation officers and others throughout the country. The Encyclopaedia of the Social Sciences contains no biography of John Augustus. The self-audit of his labors on behalf of offenders will never be regarded as of importance equal to those classics of criminology and penology, Howard's *State of the Prisons in England and Wales* (1779) and Beccaria's *Dei Delitti e delle Pene* (Crime and Punishment, 1764). But its significance in the history of society's efforts to cope with criminality cannot be gainsaid.

II

Who was this Augustus? What was he trying to accomplish? What motivated him? Very little is known of his early years, his personality and his aims that is not disclosed in his own too brief account of his work and aspirations. Fortunately, however, we have uncovered in the obscure pages of Ball Fenner's *Raising the Veil* (Boston, 1856) a journalistically vivid but instructive contemporary sketch of our hero at work:

> "Who is that fidgety old fellow, whose skin looks like a piece of brown parchment? He's here, there, and everywhere. A few moments ago I saw him wrangling with one of the officers. Now he is in earnest conversation with those females . . ."
> "That . . . is John Augustus, the philanthropist."
> "What position or office does he hold in this court?"
> "None, that I know of."
> "Does his philanthropy support him?"
> "He could answer that question himself much better than I can . . . I will introduce you to him by and by; meanwhile you had better watch his movements."
> One of the girls was now called up to the prisoner's stand. She plead guilty to the charges preferred against her.
> "I'll bail that young woman for thirty days, your Honor," cried John Augustus. "I know her parents, and very respectable people they are, too. If I can't reform her, I'll bring her into court at the expiration of that time, to be disposed of as you will."

Judge: "Mr. Clerk, you may take Mr. Augustus for bail in
the sum of thirty dollars for the prisoner's appearance here in
thirty days from this date."

When the next "unfortunate" was called up, she also plead
guilty. One of the wicked reporters was heard to remark,
"John won't bail that 'old gal,' she's too old and ugly." The
reporter was right. She was sentenced to six months imprisonment in the House of Correction. Instanter, the fountains
of her eyes were opened, and while the waters gushed forth
freely, her sobs and boohoos could be heard above the noise
within, and the rumbling of express wagons without the court
house.

The kind hearted judge was evidently moved by those tears,
and addressing the woman, he said:

"The court will give you twelve hours to leave the city. After
that time, if you are found within our precincts, or at any time
within six months next ensuing, the sentence already passed
will be executed upon you." . . . As she passed John Augustus
she saluted him with an impudent toss of the head, informing
him she was under no obligations to him, and hoped to meet
him in that uncomfortable place, the exact locality of which
has never yet been discovered, but where it is supposed by some
that tremendous fires are kept up, both night and day. . . .[1]

John can talk very rapidly. . . . He assured us that he had
more business to attend to that afternoon than any three ordinary men could manage in a fortnight. "I have got to go
down to the jail . . . and try and get a woman out who was
put in there for selling liquor—her husband was sent to the
House of Correction about three weeks ago, for the same offence—don-no whether I can get her out or not. I must go
and look after her children, anyway. She's one girl, anyway,
about seventeen years old who is very good looking—I don-no
whether she is virtuous or not, but I think more'n likely as not
she is; but I'll soon find out. Then I've got to go over to
Charlestown, and see about a girl there I bailed out the other
day—she's got into some scrape again. I don-no what it is, but
I must go and see. And then there's three or four down in
the lock-up, that I must look after."[2]

Those who come in contact with him in business matters,
and more especially in matters pertaining to courts, must expect that he will reel off more line from the end of his tongue
in fifteen minutes than any ordinary man could accomplish in
four times that space. Those who do not know him can hardly
comprehend his character and style of language, by any description that can be written. . . .[3]

I visited the house of John the philanthropist, whose surname
was Augustus. The house literally swarmed with females;
and if some of them had been fairer looking, and all of them
better clad, a stranger might have been led to suppose that he
was in a sultan's harem.

1. *Op. cit.*, pp. 32-34
2. *Id.* p. 38
3. *Id.*, note, p. 38

We were conducted into a small, well furnished room, and presently John made his appearance. . . .

He then closed the door, threw himself into an old arm-chair, and that tongue of his, which appears to be hung in the middle and oiled at each end, was immediately put into motion.

"You haint been in court today? . . . Thought not—I didn't see you there. Thirty-two simple drunks, seven common drunkards, and eight or ten larceny cases. I bailed out three, and let the rest slide. Didn't believe I could do anything with 'em —afraid to try it, anyhow. Young M——— was brought up for getting drunk, last night. I paid his fine—don-no whether he will pay me or not—guess he will, though. You know him well enough, his father keeps a store up on Cornhill—appears to be a very clever man, but I don-no much about him. I never knew the boy was dissipated before today; but you can't tell— most everybody drinks now-a-days. Some that pretend to be very temperate drink the worst."

Here a woman, who was not very young or beautiful, entered the room with a note in her hand, which she gave to the philanthropist. He laid it on the table and continued:

"This is one of my girls. I've had her here nearly a month— must take her into the court next Wednesday for sentence. One cent and costs, that's all. Must try and get her some good place to live out. Guess we can reform her, if she don't get in with her old companions again. . . ."

"I see, Mr. Augustus, you have a large number of females about your house. Are they all the unfortunate children of vice?"

"All but my own family. . . . I've got a house full, and I suppose it would be full if it was twice as large."

"And do you really support and provide for all these people, at your own expense? . . ."

"Well, not exactly . . . There are many charitable people in the city of Boston, who are willing to give for benevolent purposes when they know how and for what the funds are to be expended. If a man is taken up for drunkenness, and I pay his fine and get him discharged, he is almost sure to repay me as soon as he earns the money. It is very seldom I ever lose anything in that way."

"And what proportion of those females who are taken from houses of ill-fame, and rescued from the prisons, become reformed?"

"A great many . . . I don-no what proportion, but suppose one out of ten was reclaimed, would not that be well worth the time, labor and money that is expended on the whole? Do we not read that he who turns one sinner from the error of his ways, shall save a soul from death, and hide a multitude of sins?"[1]

Among the notables who have been in and about the Boston court house for the past twelve years, few are better known than the man John Augustus. That this man has done much good since he entered upon his career as a philanthropist, no one who

1. *Id.*, p. 41

knows anything of the subject can for a moment doubt. Many persons are of the opinion that for a few years past Mr. Augustus has done more harm than good, by bailing those who are arraigned before the courts for the commission of crimes that deserve and should receive severe punishment, and it is said that rogues have been allowed to escape through the interposition of this man.

There may be a few cases where this gentleman's philanthropy (or whatver else you please to term it) has so far outrun good judgment and discretion that it may have led him to interfere where strict justice would demand that the law should take its course. If the facts respecting such matters were fully known, methinks the public would find that where one truly guilty individual has escaped, by and with the aid of John Augustus, ten have been suffered to go at large by the connivance and direct assistance of police officers.

Mr. Augustus commenced his career as a philanthropist in 1841, in the Police Court of Boston, by bailing a man who was charged with the offence of being a common drunkard. The following year he bailed seventeen persons, all of whom were arraigned for the same offence. From that time down to the present he has continued in the laudable enterprise, and has bailed nearly five thousand people charged with this offence. Now if one out of five of this number has been reclaimed, by his interposition in their behalf, surely he has been a benefactor of mankind, and has not lived in vain.

There is one thing certainly that is praiseworthy in the character of John Augustus, and that is, he will never quarrel with any person on account of his political opinions or religious belief; neither will he express his own, even when urged to do so. By pursuing this course he is, like the Apostle Paul, enabled to make himself "all things to all men," believing that by so doing he can "*save some.*"

There are but few men to be found who would, if they had been placed in precisely his situation, have stood the ordeal of public opinion of those who stand high in the community as the most charitable and beneficent citizens. I believe that whenever and wherever he has made mistakes, in his impetuous zeal in laboring for the good of others, it has been the fault of the head, and not the heart.

The engraving of Mr. Augustus which may be found in this work is a tolerably fair representation of the man, although not so correct as it should be.[1]

From this vivid sketch we can to a great extent reconstruct in our imagination the man and his work. It is not hard to picture him as a sort of dynamic synthesis of Paul Revere, John Howard and Florence Nightingale, as he rode back and forth in his "chaise," animated by an unquenchable thirst for justice tempered with kindness and understanding.

1. *Id.*, pp. 282-284. (See frontispiece)

I resolved to adopt a new mode of traveling, and therefore
bought a horse and chaise. I employed him a large portion of
every day; I have used the same animal to the present time,
and he appears to be pretty familiar with every part of the
city; the jail and the court house have been his usual stopping
places; one chaise after another has done excellent service, and
become worthless; three have already been worn out, and the
fourth is now in requisition. I have traveled 15,000 miles within
the limits of the city; 4,000 women have been conveyed in my
carriages to and from various parts of the city. (p. 24)

It may be that Augustus was a little touched by fanaticism,
but his was the zeal of one doing a humanitarian work in the
face of great obstacles. The same arguments leveled against
probation work today were thrown at him. In addition he
had to meet the opposition of certain court officers.

Throughout his activities, as Augustus points out, he worked
as a volunteer receiving no compensation for his efforts and
moved only by the urge to help his less fortunate fellowmen.
His method was to bail the offender after conviction, to utilize
this favor as an entering wedge to the convict's confidence
and friendship, and through such evidences of friendliness
as helping the offender to obtain a job and aiding his family
in various ways, to drive the wedge home. When the defendant
was later brought into court for sentence, Augustus would
report on his progress toward reformation, and the judge
would usually fine the convict one cent and costs, instead of
committing him to an institution. Augustus, with "that
tongue of his, which appears to be hung in the middle and
oiled at each end," must have been a most convincing advocate, for owing to his efforts it before long became the rule
of the Boston police court that an offender, if bailed "on
probation," was released on very small surety and if at the
expiration of the assigned time the defendant was reported
to be reformed, the penalty for the offence was the nominal
fine. Illustrations of Augustus' procedure in court and the
superiority of some of his views regarding the judicial disposition of cases are to be found in pages 19-23 of his report.

In the case of drunkards Augustus insisted upon the convict "taking the pledge," which (according to his account)

seems to have had a more magical effect upon chronic alcoholics than a similar ceremony has today. Inducing the defendant to take the pledge or "promise not to drink liquor" is still a favorite and easy method of "probation work" in certain courts.

The home of Augustus seems to have been a sort of clearing-house for the trials and tribulations of offenders and their families, as is indicated both in the account quoted and in Augustus' own report. If only the personal nature of the contacts with probationers, so quaintly described by Augustus, could have been retained with the progress of probation work, it could today boast of much more effective effort than it can be credited with. It is just as true today as it was in the days of Augustus and it has been throughout the ages, that the essence of "the art of helping people out of trouble" is a humanitarian-animated friendship guided by insight and understanding.

There are certain conflicting attitudes toward social work in general and the supervision of probationers in particular. One group, mistaking easy sentimentalism for intelligence-guided sentiment, either resorts to threats or insists on the old-fashioned methods of "charity." The other camp, having just gotten science as some people get religion, believes that all warm human contact with clients must be shunned as "unscientific." Both attitudes are unsound. Technical proficiency is very necessary in probation as well as other forms of social work; but so are a ripe humanitarianism and a philosophy of life. Neither undisciplined emotionalism nor machine-like "technique" will in itself obtain desirable results. The daily duties of the probation officer must express an ethics as well as an economics of philanthropy.

After two years of work Augustus passed from the supervision of drunkards to efforts with other adult offenders and juvenile delinquents. Without the assistance of a psychiatric clinic and social workers, he seems to have accomplished much good. Certainly his contact with children was more sympathetic and sometimes more understanding than that of some probation officers of a number of so-called juvenile courts today. (pp. 13, 34)

It is significant that the first probation officer was careful to make thorough investigations of candidates for release on probation, recognizing the need of a careful selection of persons suited to that particular form of corrective treatment and assistance:

> Great care was observed of course, to ascertain whether the prisoners were promising subjects for probation, and to this end it was necessary to take into consideration the previous character of the person, his age and the influences by which he would in future be likely to be surrounded, and although these points were not rigidly adhered to, still they were the circumstances which usually determined my action. In such cases of probation it was agreed on my part, that I would note their general conduct, see that they were sent to school or supplied with some honest employment, and that I should make an impartial report to the court; whenever they should desire it. (p. 34)

Even today there are so-called probation offices in which only a very sketchy investigation is made, and indeed in many cases there are not even elementary data on hand regarding men placed on probation.

The activities of our pioneer probation officer were not limited to court appearances. They anticipated the practice of temporary detention of certain types of accused persons in private homes, hospitals and other suitable places. (pp. 36, 43) In this day, when the problem of placing delinquent children in foster homes is so important, it is of interest to read with what understanding and sympathy Augustus "placed out" the young delinquents whom he first took charge of. (pp.14,42)

Nor must it be assumed that once his clients were out on bail nothing further was done with or for them. In this respect also the work of Augustus was superior to that found in certain probation offices down to this day. Some of them offer little in the way of oversight of probationers. Perfunctory, sporadic office "check-ups" are certainly no adequate substitute for the preparation of a plan of treatment and rehabilitation and for guidance of probationers in carrying out the plan. In one year, Augustus reports, he made no fewer than "1,500 calls and received more than this number at my house." On certain aspects of supervisory work the Norfolk County committee, memorializing the legislature for the establishment of an asylum for alcoholics, pointed out that, "to say nothing of the formalities and liabilities which belong, alike, to all courts of law, he has, in most cases, provided a temporary home for his fallen brother, and allowed no rest to his head until he has done his utmost to procure for him employment." Yet despite this all important feature of supervisory activity which the pioneer probation worker engaged in, many a probation officer today still doubts whether aid in the obtaining of employment for probationers is a legitimate part of probation work! In this, as in other respects indicated, modern probation officers need to go back to the experience of this "humble mechanic" who at the very beginning of probation set certain standards which not a few probation offices have not yet reached.

These rehabilitative efforts by John Augustus were inspired not only by a strong humanitarian impulse but by a definite view that "the object of the law is to reform criminals, and to prevent crime and not to punish maliciously, or from a spirit of revenge." (p. 23) Yet this eminently practical view of the aims of politically organized society in dealing with offenders must even at this late date still be defended against the shortsighted rationalizations of those who administer a questionable "justice" on the basis of vengefulness.

III

Augustus in the 1840's was more careful to avail himself of any technical means for the improvement of his work than many probation officers are today. When one considers the shabby condition of probation records in not a few of the criminal courts of this country, he must marvel at the intelligence and foresight evidenced by Augustus a hundred years ago. He "preserved a careful record of every case in which he has interested himself, and he is thus enabled to furnish an intelligent account of a large portion of the persons who, by his means, have been saved. . . ." Two very interesting records, in the form of long rolls in which various pertinent data have been entered, have by good fortune come into possession of the Harvard Law School Library and are preserved among its treasures. We reproduce parts of these first probation records. (Figs. 1-6)

The first roll appears to be in the handwriting of John Augustus, and "Shoes the number bail'd at both courts (police and municipal) together with amount of bail 5 Years Ending Oct. 1848."[1] (Figs. 1 and 2) It was probably this to which the legislative committee, charged with considering the advisability of creating an asylum for drunkards, referred in the following words:

> A roll was exhibited to the committee, containing the names and places of residence of the three hundred men and women who had been saved by the untiring and disinterested philanthropy of Mr. Augustus, . . . with the date of the conviction, the time to which sentence was deferred, and the sum finally paid in each case; and it was impossible to look without emotion upon such a record of the unpretending but noble labors of a single man in the cause of humanity and virtue. Among the names of the benefactors of their race, few deserve a higher place than that of John Augustus; and in the day when God shall judge men 'according to the deeds done in the body,' when 'they that turn many to righteousness shall shine as the stars forever and ever,' that record will confer upon it an honor more enduring than attaches to many of the proudest achievements of statesmen or warriors. (p. 32)

The second roll, "written and copied (with few exceptions) from the *Court Records* by *William Mills, January 1855,*" lists the dates, names, addresses, record numbers, amounts of bail and costs of offenders in the Boston police and municipal

1. The writer has tried to obtain specimens of the handwriting of John Augustus to compare with that of the roll, but without success. Chief Justice Wilfred Bolster of the Boston municipal court kindly consented to have the files of the Boston police court searched for the period during which Augustus was active, but this disclosed no memoranda or correspondence in the handwriting of John Augustus.

courts who were bailed by John Augustus from 1841 to 1855.[1]
(Figs. 3-6) This second roll is more complete than the first but
contains many of the names of the former. (Compare Figs. 1
and 3, for example.)

Still further evidence of Augustus' creativity is furnished
by his various suggestions for needed reforms. For example,
he seems to have anticipated most of those who recognize the
need of some such official as a public defender to aid the poor
in their defense against criminal charges:

> I became considerably acquainted with the prisoners, their
> offences, their wants and condition, and occasionally found
> those arraigned who had little cause to hope for justice by rea-
> son of their poverty and ignorance, in opposition to the power,
> experience and learning of the prosecuting attorney. Often I
> would find a very youthful prisoner, who was arraigned for the
> first time in his life, and who was never before within the walls
> of a court house; destitute of friends to advise, or money to pro-
> cure counsel, which means, if within their power, might perhaps,
> establish the proof of their innocence . . . I thought it as much
> a duty to have the temple of justice watched, and to inquire
> who was imprisoned that should go free.

There are many who to this day are shocked at the need of
having "the temple of justice watched." They fondly believe
that as soon as a human being becomes a judge he is magically
transformed into a Solomon. Long before the modern interest
in the psychology of judicial decision, our observant cobbler
had this to say:

> If my observations have been correct, I have found that
> wrong customs prevail sometimes in courts of justice as well as
> in communities, and that the minds of the dispensers of justice
> may occasionally be biased in favor or against a prisoner, by
> the external circumstances by which he may be surrounded; in
> view of that state of things I resolved to bail some of the pit-
> iable objects whenever prudence might dictate. (pp. 17, 38)

Ever alert to propose improvements of the existing treatment of social misfits, Augustus encouraged the establishment

1. Although it was claimed by the inhabitants of Norfolk County who
memorialized the legislature in behalf of an asylum for chronic alcoholics
that "fully three-fourths" of the 232 alcoholics bailed by Augustus from
1841 to 1845 were by 1845 "temperate and orderly citizens . . . gaining a
respectable livelihood," we have been unable to discover any follow-up records
kept by Augustus from which such a conclusion might have been drawn. But
from the tireless enthusiasm and activity of the man, we should not be surprised if such a record was kept by him.

of "an asylum . . . for the drunkard." A good deal that is
contained in the memorial to the legislature for the establishment of such an institution is as pertinent today as it was
in 1845, particularly this sentence: "It is believed that the
largest portion of this class (misguided persons who so frequently render themselves obnoxious to the laws by the vice
of intemperance) who are, according to our present laws,
now locked up in jails and houses of correction, and lost to
their families, to society, and to themselves, may be restored
to usefulness and respectability by the establishment of a state
asylum expressly devoted to their cure." (p. 25)

Even to what might be called family welfare work—with
the non-criminal—Augustus made his contribution. By 1846
his fame among the poor and wretched was so great that "a
new avenue seemed to be opened; a great many females, young
and old, whom I had not seen at court, called upon me to ask
assistance in some form or other." Thus this Boston cobbler,
like Hans Sachs, the *Meistersinger* shoemaker of old Nürnberg,
was called upon to spend more and more of his wisdom and
humanitarian impulse in the service of his neighbors. Placing
out of children into suitable homes, giving temporary shelter
to various afflicted adults, finding employment for them, doing
single-handed the work of a dozen social welfare agencies was
the inevitable fate of Augustus.

IV

If John Augustus' labors had met with little opposition
they would still deserve an important place in the story of
penology. All the more do they evoke our admiration when
one considers the obstacles under which he had to labor. (p.37)
One cannot but admire the firm fearlessness and determina-
tion of the man. In an age when some judges and court
officers "clothed with a little brief authority" were perhaps
more than today conscious of their great importance in the
scheme of things, Augustus stuck to his guns and politely but
firmly corrected the court when he was convinced that the
right was on his side. (pp. 9-11)

By 1843 he had extended his activities to the municipal court, where he again "met with much opposition from the officers when they discovered the nature of my labors," although the judges and sheriff were by that time "by no means unfavorable" to his efforts. Here again the simple singleness of purpose and deep-rooted faith of the man in his work are disclosed. He was at first "rudely expelled without the least cause" from the seats of the mighty, when he attempted to take his place in the enclosure reserved for members of the bar in order to represent the interests of his charges more effectively. But where a lesser man would have given up after an annoying series of rebuffs, this was the reaction of our irrepressible probation worker: "I always endeavored to keep myself as cool and as calm as possible under such treatment, keeping my object constantly in view." (p. 16) Indeed, he even turned such setbacks to good account in his work: "By being driven back I was not unfrequently brought in contiguity with the prisoner's dock, so that I could easily converse with the prisoner and this was the very object I desired. . . . Here then, were two points gained,—to take my place with the members of the bar, and to occasionally whisper a word of hope to the desponding heart of some unfortunate and perhaps innocent person." (p. 16) Throughout these and similar experiences Augustus, with the unfailing confidence of a prophet, made up his mind "that the spirit of the opposition sprung from envy, hatred, ill-will and strife, and must therefore, be overcome with good." (p. 18)

Another interesting passage in John Augustus' report illustrates the traditional difference in point of view between the prosecutor charged with "disposing" of cases as rapidly as possible—with "keeping the docket clear"—and the social worker, for whom the mere imposition of sentence is far from a solution of the problems involved in any case. In 1846 Augustus became surety for a number of juveniles. He writes:

> By a decision of the court upon my motion, the cases of these children were to be continued, but the question of the term of continuance caused considerable discussion. I always urged a protracted continuance, but Mr. Parker (the prose-

cutor) was extremely anxious to have the cases disposed of as early as possible. I wished ample time to test the promises of these youths to behave well in future. Judge Cushing was disposed to allow such cases to stand continued from term to term, and if at the expiration of a certain period, a good report was given of their behavior during the time they had been on probation, their sentences were very light. (p. 33)

Nor was such opposition the only kind Augustus met with. The reader will find in his report an exposé of that peculiarly obnoxious form of selfishness that feeds on the misfortunes and friendlessness of offenders against the law. In his early naiveté Augustus "could not imagine the cause of this unfriendly spirit" that he met with on the part of police officers and the clerks of courts, not until he learned "that for every drunkard whom I bailed the officer was actually losing seventy-five cents, to which he would have been entitled if the case had been otherwise disposed of," was the true motive disclosed. It appears that for the service of each *mittimus* to the House of Correction an officer "earned" a few cents. This petty graft is still grown, albeit on another branch of the tree of justice; the swollen profits made by some sheriffs in "keeping" and underfeeding petty offenders are still a legitimate form of publicly sanctioned blood money in some parts of the country. And profits are still being made by private contractors out of the labor of prisoners. Is it any wonder that many offenders, who have any intelligence at all, are inclined to regard the sacred precincts of justice as too frequently the poaching grounds of hypocritical officials of little better morality, but better fortune, than themselves?

The reader will find many other penetrating criticisms of the administration of criminal justice in the interesting report of John Augustus. He was a keen observer and fearless critic and many of his observations are valid today.

V

The Emperor Augustus was the founder of the powerful Roman Empire. John Augustus was the founder of an empire of social service that has rapidly spread its wholesome influence not only in America but in other quarters of the globe. Every state in the Union has a probation law applying to children, with the exception of Wyoming. Maine and Wyoming have no juvenile court laws but Maine has juvenile probation. Forty states, the District of Columbia, and Canada have adult probation laws as well as juvenile; (only eight states have no adult probation). The most recent national Directory of Probation Officers lists 4920 probation officers serving the courts in the United States and Canada. Of these, 3985 are regularly salaried officers. There are 2179 counties out of a total of 3516 in the United States which now have probation officers.

In Europe, also, probation is making considerable progress, although there reliance still seems to be largely on volunteer, non-professional workers.

But despite the spread of probation laws, we are still essentially at the stage of extensive rather than intensive culture of this promising and relatively economical type of correctional work. The next stage of development must be marked by a widespread effort to cultivate the soil of probation more intelligently and intensively. This can be done through the conscious evaluation of various arts and sciences (*e.g.*, social case work, psychology, mental hygiene, education, and the like) for their possible contributions to the master art of rehabilitating delinquents and criminals. In the meantime the probation and parole officer can derive much aid and comfort from the chronicle of the pioneer labors of staunch and fearless John Augustus.

SHELDON GLUECK

Cambridge, Massachusetts
March 1939

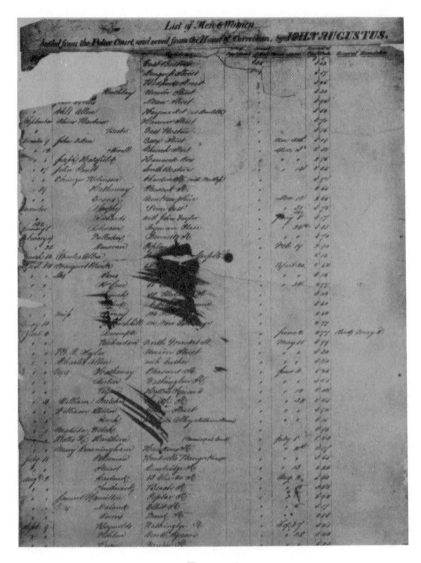

FIGURE 1

Beginning of the roll of probationers from the Boston Police Court, supervised by John Augustus from 1841 through 1854.

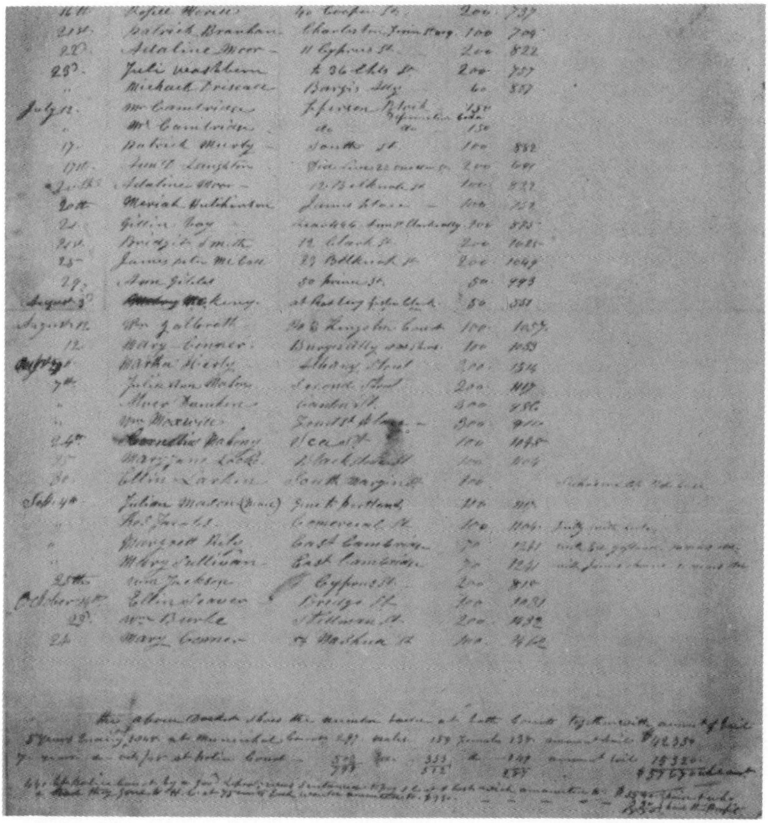

FIGURE 2

End of the roll of probationers from the Boston Municipal Court, supervised by John Augustus 1843 through 1854. The final paragraph reads:

the above Docket shoes the number bailed at both Courts together with amount of bail
5 years ending Oct. 1848 at Municipal Court 297, Males 159, Females 138, amount bail $42350
7 years   do – Oct./48   at Police Court   502,   do– 353   do – 149 amount bail 15320.

799   512   287 $57670 Whole
                                                                      Amt.

440, at Police Court by a good Report, were sentenced to pay 1 cent & costs which amounted to
                                                                      $1540 (paid & who
& had they gone to H. C. at 75 cents Each would have amounted to $330. –   330 (had this profit

$1870

The following list contains the names of persons bailed at the Municipal and Police Courts of Boston in the

County of Suffolk

by

John Augustus.

in thirteen years ending December 30th 1854. Those in the Police Court were complained of mostly as common drunkards. In the Municipal Court for various offences.

The Police Court

Dates	Names	Residence			
		1841			
Dec. 21	James Vayle	East Boston	1113	30	3 13
	Charles Allen	Hanmaker's	1117	30	3 13
21	John Butt	East Boston	1176	30	3 11
Aug. 11	Oliver Barbour	Hanover St.	1318	30	3 70
21	James Downing	Congress St.	1320	30	3 31
16	John Hollis	Flan St.	1471	30	3 94
Dec. 1	George Osborn	Bedford St.	2219	30	3 31
	Samuel Brothbay	Union St.	1833	30	3 30
9	William Askew	Essex St.	1723	30	3 07
13	Nath. Powell	Church St.	1931	30	4 30
31	Joseph Hatfield	Hancock Row	2033	30	2 71
27	John Gault	South Boston		30	4 13
	Ebenezer Robinson		2041	30	3 94
30	William Hathaway	Pleasant St.	2029	30	2 65
	Reuben Evans	New Hampshire	2029	30	2 65
1	Cornelius Murphy	Down East	2011	30	3 71
	William Richards	with John Sayler	2216	30	5 17
		1842		570	4 57

FIGURE 3

Beginning of a copy of the court record of probationers from the Boston Police Court from 1841 through 1854. Copied by William Mills in January 1855.

Nov 9 Peter Small   Lancaster St.   7223 30 Drun 6 8 45
"   Mc Coroty   Hamilton St.   7591 30 Oct 29
Dec 24 Margaret McLaughlin Washington Place 1571 200 Paid 6 more from bill &c.
" 26 Thomas Goudty   Prince St.   7745 30 Jan 7&45

Total number of Persons bailed _ 654
"   Amount of bail _ _ _ $24570

The Municipal Court for various offences

Date	Names	Residence	No. of Cont Recd	Amt of Bail
		1843		
April 14	Hannah Diamond	Endicott St.	991	70
" 24	Mc Reed	Commercial St.		50
Nov 25	George Lawrence	Friend St.	313	200
Dec 15	D. D.	" "	313	200
		1844		320
March 13	Lysander Ripley	at Boutelles	348	100
April 9	M. C. Windman	South Boston	444	100
" "	Thomas Windman	" "	444	100
" 11	Elizabeth Reper	" "	409	100
" "	Betsy Rohan	" "		100
" 18	Michael Murphy	Ann St.	443	200
May 13	Isaac May	Pearl St.	576	100
" "	Edward Sang		576	100
" 14	Maria Kauffer		584	100
" 18	Michael Murphy	Ann St.	443	30
" 28	John Siland		35	50
June 7	Mary Ann Laws	Kind St.	613	100
" 18	Isaac May	Karl St.	576	100

FIGURE 4

End of the copy of the court record of probationers from the Boston Police Court and beginning of a similar record from the Boston Municipal Court.

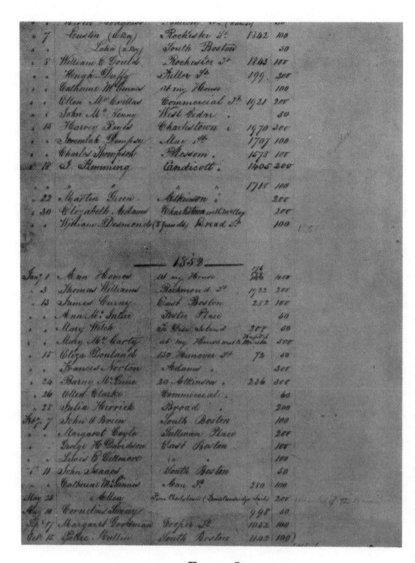

FIGURE 5

Continuation of the record from the Boston Municipal Court.
Note children listed.

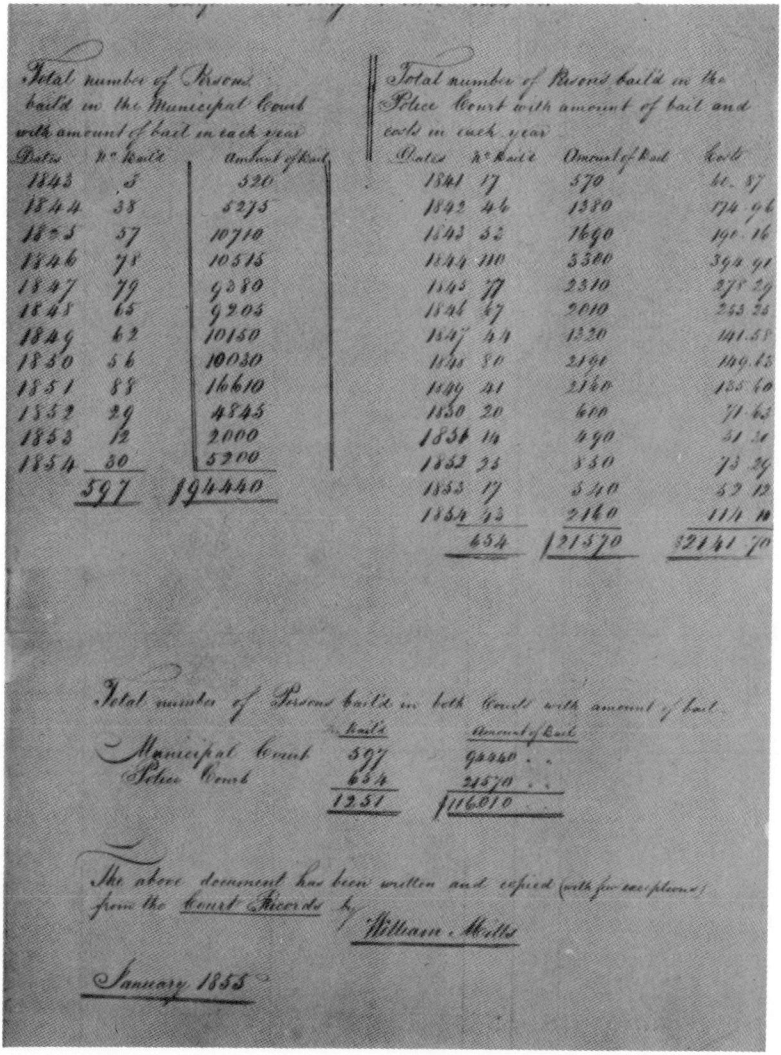

Total number of Persons bail'd in the Municipal Court with amount of bail in each year

Dates	No. bail'd	Amount of bail
1843	5	520
1844	38	5275
1845	57	10710
1846	78	10515
1847	79	9380
1848	65	9205
1849	62	10150
1850	56	10030
1851	88	16610
1852	29	4845
1853	12	2000
1854	30	5200
	597	$94440

Total number of Persons bail'd in the Police Court with amount of bail and costs in each year

Dates	No. bail'd	Amount of bail	Costs
1841	17	570	60.87
1842	46	1380	174.96
1843	52	1690	190.16
1844	110	5300	394.91
1845	77	2310	278.29
1846	67	2010	253.25
1847	44	1320	141.58
1848	80	2190	149.15
1849	41	2140	135.60
1850	20	600	71.65
1851	14	490	51.30
1852	25	850	73.29
1853	17	540	52.12
1854	43	2160	114.10
	654	$21570	$2141.70

Total number of Persons bail'd in both Courts with amount of bail

	No. bail'd	Amount of bail
Municipal Court	597	94440 . .
Police Court	654	21570 . .
	1251	$116010 . .

The above document has been written and copied (with few exceptions) from the Court Records by

William Mills

January 1855

FIGURE 6

End of the record of William Mills with summary of cases bailed to John Augustus from 1841 through 1854.

A REPORT

OF THE

LABORS OF JOHN AUGUSTUS,

FOR THE LAST TEN YEARS,

IN AID OF THE UNFORTUNATE:

CONTAINING

A DESCRIPTION OF HIS METHOD OF OPERATIONS; STRIKING IN-
CIDENTS, AND OBSERVATIONS UPON THE IMPROVEMENT OF
SOME OF OUR CITY INSTITUTIONS, WITH A VIEW TO THE
BENEFIT OF THE PRISONER AND OF SOCIETY.

PUBLISHED BY REQUEST.

"Ambition is a lottery, where, however uneven the chances, there are some prizes;
but in dissipation every one draws a blank."—MONTAGUE.

BOSTON:

WRIGHT & HASTY, PRINTERS,

No. 3 WATER STREET.

1852.

[facsimile of original title page]

REPORT.

By request of my friends to whom I have been under the greatest obligations for the last few years, I now with diffidence yet with much self-gratification, present a brief yet comprehensive report of a portion of my labors for the last ten consecutive years. It is generally known that my time has been wholly devoted to the unfortunate, in seeking out the wretched who have become victims to their passions and subjects of punishment by law, and that my mission has been to raise the fallen, reform the criminal, and so far as my humble abilities would allow, to transform the abode of suffering and misery to the home of happiness; a brief account of the manner in which my efforts have been put forth, will I trust afford satisfaction to those of my friends who have contributed their means and their encouragement of my labors, and thus enabled me to accomplish what by the blessing of heaven, I have done, yet what I could at first never even have hoped to accomplish.— I have spent the greater part of my time at the Jail, the Court House, and in the abodes of the unfortunate, and those charged with all kinds of offences against the law, with a view to ameliorate their condition, and to effect their reformation; and here let me say that the amount of labor which I have performed in the courts alone, in the specified time, is infinitely greater than I at first believed it in my power to accomplish, and to my friends it will not appear like boasting or self-praise if I give a plain transcript of facts as I have recorded them. Every one who has the *will* to do, may do a vast amount of good in the cause in which I am engaged.

In the first place, I will answer the questions which are frequently asked as to how I receive compensation, and how I am able to bail so many, and how I manage to look to the cases of so many persons. I devote my time daily, and often a large portion of the night, in the performance of the various labors which fall within my province. I am no agent for any sect, society, or association whatever. I receive no salary, neither have I ever received a dollar for any service as a salary, nor do I know of any individual who ever became responsible for me, even to the amount of a dollar; I am therefore not accountable to any sect, society or individual for the manner in which my efforts have been applied.

I put my hand to the plough in 1841, in the Police Court, the scene of my earliest efforts to reform the drunkard, which acts on my part were wholly voluntary and have been so to the present time, and equally voluntary have those acted who have aided me to prosecute effectually the work I began.

I cannot better describe my mode of action in the Police Court than by introducing an every-day scene there. It was at this time that the great Washingtonian Temperance reform was exciting the attention of the public mind, and when a general interest pervaded the hearts of the philanthropic, to liberate the wretched inebriate from the prison of his own destructive vice, and to loose the bonds which held him captive, by removing from him the pernicious influences by which he had been surrounded, and by causing him to feel that he was still a man.

In the month of August, 1841, I was in court one morning, when the door communicating with the lock-room was opened and an officer entered, followed by a ragged and wretched looking man, who took his seat upon the bench allotted to prisoners. I imagined from the man's appearance, that his offence was that of yielding to his appetite for intoxicating drinks, and in a few moments I found that my suspicions were correct, for the clerk read the complaint, in which the man was charged with being a common drunkard. The case was clearly made out, but before sentence had been passed, I conversed with him for a few moments, and found that he was not yet past all hope of reformation, although his appearance and his looks precluded a belief in the minds of others that he would ever become a *man* again. He told me that if he could be saved from the House of Correction, he never again would taste intoxicating liquors; there was such an earnestness in that tone, and a look expressive of firm resolve, that I determined to aid him; I bailed him, by permission of the Court. He was ordered to appear for sentence in three weeks from that time. He signed the pledge and became a sober man; at the expiration of this period of probation, I accompanied him into the court room; his whole appearance was changed and no one, not even the scrutinizing officers, could have believed that he was the same person who less than a month before, had stood trembling on the prisoner's stand.— The Judge expressed himself much pleased with the account we gave of the man, and instead of the usual penalty,—imprisonment in the House of Correction,—he fined him one *cent* and costs, amounting in all to $3,76, which was immediately paid. The man continued industrious and sober, and without doubt has been by this treatment, saved from a drunkard's grave.

This was truly encouraging, and before January, 1842, I had bailed seventeen persons for a similar offence, and they had severally been sentenced in the same manner, which in all amounted to $60,87. Eleven of this number paid the fine, but the other six being too poor to raise the amount, I paid it for them.

It became a rule of this court, that a person charged with being a common drunkard, if bailed on probation, the amount of the bail should be thirty dollars, and if at the expiration of the time assigned, the person reformed, the penalty for the offence was the payment of a fine of one *cent* and costs of court.

Out of the number whom I bailed that year, I now recollect

the residence of but one, for a change of circumstances has in many cases called some of the number to various parts of the country, and several have doubtless paid the debt of nature, but so far as I have been able to ascertain, they have sacredly kept the pledge which they were then induced to take. The person to whom I here allude lives on Commercial street, in this city, and sustains an excellent character, as a sober man and a good citizen. In an interview with this man about a month since, I remembered a remark which was made to me by a well known clergyman of this city,* about the time he was bailed; he said, "If one drunkard out of fifty could be saved from drunkenness and restored to the bosom of his family, it would more than pay for all the labor expended in attempting to restore the other forty-nine." This language which has been thus demonstrated, gave me great encouragement. Soon after this man was bailed, the clergyman to whom I have referred called at my shop, in Franklin Avenue, and informed me that there was a man in an alley near Haymarket Square, who was very drunk, and unable to walk; he requested me to go and take care of him. I expressed my fears that he might be taken to jail by the officers before we could find him, but he offered to go with me and assist me. This offer I thought very extraordinary, for here was a clergyman *actually* going "out into the highway and hedges." Another gentleman who was present volunteered to accompany us. It was quite dark when we arrived at the spot, and groping our way about, we found the man lying upon the ground; we endeavored to urge him to leave his cold lodgings and to follow us, but he refused, and we led him from the place. We carried him to a Hotel, but at first they refused to allow him to remain in the house, giving as a reason, that he did not get his liquor there. The next morning he was conveyed to his home in Waltham.

I have related this as an instance of *practical* preaching; this act of the Rev. gentleman was a noble one, and if the clergy of all denominations would preach in this way a little

* Rev. Mr. Lathrop.

more than they do, I am confident that a much greater amount of good would be accomplished than now is. I had labored about a year when it became evident that much good had been and might be performed, by laboring in the field in which I had commenced operations, and to promote this object, several kind and philanthropic individuals placed in my hands donations of various sums, which enabled me to accomplish a much greater amount of good than I could have done from my own limited means alone. In 1842 I continued to attend the court and to bail as many as I could attend to, those whom I believed might be benefited by such acts on my part; but here I found my efforts materially cramped, and in some measure limited, for my business affairs of course, claimed a share of my attention, as I was at that time engaged in the boot-making business, in Franklin Avenue, near the court house. I generally went into court about half past nine in the morning, thinking to return to my shop in a short time, but very frequently found it impossible to leave the court room till twelve or one o'clock, as I waited to bail some unfortunate person; this course broke in upon my business engagements at my shop, and the delay which caused the evil arose in most cases, from the opposition of the officers of the court to my mode of operation, and in some cases when I left the court room for a few moments, the unhappy object whose welfare was my aim, would be examined, and sentenced before my return. I resolved not to be frustrated in this manner, and thus sacrificed much valuable time.

I continued on in this way for some time, and found that occasions rapidly multiplied where I was called upon to bail the prisoner, and to counsel and aid the wretched. It soon became generally known in the city that I was saving drunkards from the House of Correction, and daily calls upon my attention were increased; my business at my shop suffered sadly by neglect. In August, 1842, I found that I had bailed thirty persons.

Scarcely an hour in the day elapsed, but some one would call at my house or my shop and tell their tale of sorrow;

one had a husband who had been arrested by the police, another a wife who had been dragged to the watch house; she had perhaps, been taken out of bed at midnight and hurried away from her babe and her family. This was accompanied by a request for me to bail her, or him. The unhappy person might add, "I work for Mr. B., we have four small children; my wife is a very good woman, and her only fault is, that she drinks once in a while. If you will only get her off, I will pay you any thing you may ask." Scarcely perhaps, had the person paused, when a poor woman would enter to tell me that her husband, who drinks a little once in a while, went out last night and had not returned; she watched for him all night and had just learned that he had been arrested, and taken to jail. She would close by saying, "Do, Mr. Augustus, go and get him out and let me return to my babe. Will you say yes? What shall I do? they will carry him to the House of Correction," the pair stand importuning me, and as I rise from my bench, there enters a little girl who can hardly speak for crying; after some kind words, the little one says, "Mr. Augustus, mother wants to have you come down to our house. Father is in jail. Mr. Stratton took him away last night. Mother is very sick and can't go out." I can do no less than to tell the little one to run home and assure her mother that I will come, and aid her all in my power, and having thus driven the tears back that had begun to flow, the little one trips away to give joy to her mother.

Similar cases were constantly occurring. I would carefully note their names and residences; then go to the court and watch perhaps for hours, till some one whose name I had entered, was brought in from the lock-up, and would then make an effort to save him.

Frequently I suffered extreme inconvenience from the opposition of the police officers as well as the clerk of this court. I could not imagine the cause of this unfriendly spirit, until I learned that for every drunkard whom I bailed, the officer was actually losing seventy-five cents, to which he would have been entitled if the case had been otherwise disposed of; this in the aggregate, amounted to quite a sum, as will be seen from a glance at the table of statistics, but for all that, I believed that generally, a drunkard could more effectually be reformed by kindness, than by imprisonment in the House of Correction.

I cannot better give the reader an idea of some of the troubles which I had to encounter, than to extract an article from the *Boston Daily Mail.*

"Bridget H., a middle aged, long visaged woman, in a black hood and red shawl, with as much dirt as sorrow upon her pale face, was complained of by police officer Fuller for being a common drunkard. She listened to the reading of the complaint, and in answer to the usual question by the clerk, " are you guilty or not guilty ?"

Bridget. Not guilty; I never was a drunkard."

Mr. Fuller. I found her last night intoxicated, and have seen her so before.

Bridget. No; you never saw me drunk. You said I was so once, and threatened to take me to the watch house, and I gave you a silver half dollar to let me go. You would not have taken me this time if I had had silver to hire you to let me alone.

Justice Cushing. Mr. Fuller, how is this?

Fuller. It is not true—the woman will say what she pleases, and I cannot help it.

[Officer V., to ease his brother constable from an awkward position, came forward and stated to the court that the woman was not to be believed, having been in the House of Correction.]

Bridget. I never was in the House of Correction *but once* in *my life.*

His Honor here understood the woman to say, " I never was there in my life," and he replied, "that's false, I have your name here as an old offender, and your charge against the officer is not to be accredited a moment after this denial."

Mr. John Augustus, who was present, and standing near the prisoner, mildly observed, " she said, your Honor, that she had been in the House of Correction *once.*"

Justice. She did not say so,—I heard what the woman said, that *she never was in the House of Correction in her life.*

Police Officer. That is true, your Honor, she said so.

John Augustus—(warmly), But I say she did *not* say so! I heard the words she used, and I appeal to the spectators.

Considerable excitement began to manifest itself among the few spectators of this highly dignified dispute, and several voices exclaimed, "She did not say so,—Augustus is right!" In fact there were not three persons present but heard Bridget distinctly admit that she had been in the House of Correction once.

Officer. Silence in the court!

Justice—(with temper), Mr. Augustus, hold your tongue, sir! Sit down, or I'll direct an officer to take you out of the room!

Augustus. I *will* say what I heard.

Justice. (Rising with a *show* of dignity), you can't say any thing! take a seat, instantly sir! (The incorrigible philanthropist seated himself, and the justice readjusted his spectacles.) Sir, you intrude upon the patience of the court; you contradict me, and appeal to the spectators, as though I did not know what was said as well as they. (Augustus rising,) keep your seat and be silent, or I'll have you taken out of the room. What right have you to interfere in a question of veracity between a highly respectable officer, so far as I know, and this woman?

Augustus. But I wish to explain the —

Justice. Not another word, sir! (To the prisoner,) Bridget, are you married?

Bridget. Yes; but I don't live with my husband.

An officer. Her husband is a steady man and works in Roxbury; but she is so bad he cannot live with her.

Justice. Ah, I see his name, *he has been up three or four times for beating his wife.*

*   *   *   *   *   *   *

(*To the Clerk.*) Say four months.

Clerk. Bridget H———, the court sentences you to four months imprisonment in the House of Correction."

Again, in July, 1842, another instance occurred, the mention of which will suffice for this court. I went down to the lock-up (beneath the Court House) to see a man whom I intended to bail that day, and when passing along the main passage leading to the cells, a woman who was imprisoned called to me and requested me to bail her. I told her I could not, when she asked, why I could not aid her as well as to aid men; she said she had a husband and children, and expressed much regret for her conduct, and a desire to be allowed to return home. The officer, Mr. D———, who was then a constable of the court, was quīte angry and ordered me to leave the place and go about my business ; and as I had never bailed a woman, I declined doing so now and left the place, though with a feeling of regret that I had not offered her at least, a word of encouragement and hope. As I was returning home revolving in my mind the scenes of the morning, I met a friend, and related the incident to him ; the next time I met this man, which was but an hour afterwards, he informed me that he had related the affair to his wife, who expressed a desire to save the poor creature, and even offered to take her into her family, that she might be able to watch over and encourage her, but it was too late, the case had been disposed of, and the woman sentenced; as I parted with him I could but remark that if ladies generally possessed hearts like hers, few there would be who would suffer for sympathy, advice, or aid.

I made up my mind hereafter to recognize "Woman's Rights," and that the very next woman who applied to me to bail her,—if I found her a worthy object of aid—I would do it, in spite of all the *Rum-breaths* and the seventy-five cent fees of the Police Court, provided that the Judge would give his consent.

On the 27th of July, of this year, a woman who was engaged in the Washingtonian cause, called on me and requested me to go to the court and bail a woman in whom she felt an active interest. She said the family resided in Eliot street, and her husband was in the employment of Mr. H—— D. P——, near Court Square. I promised to investigate the case further, and accordingly called to see her husband, who was employed at the restaurant, but a few rods from my shop.— He appeared to be a very kind hearted man, and spoke in terms of the most tender regard of his erring wife, and with deepest emotion told me that he was willing to sacrifice every thing he had in the world, if the reformation of his wife could be effected. He also expressed a desire that the matter might be kept as secret as possible. I went over to court to watch the moving of the waters, which hitherto had borne all drunkards on its current down to the abyss of destruction and despair. When the woman was brought up, I attempted to whisper a few words of hope to her, but I was rudely ordered away by the officers, and the complaint was read to the woman, in which she was charged with being a common drunkard; the witnesses were called; the testimony was strongly against her and the case was fully made out. Just before sentence was pronounced, I told the Justice that I would, with his consent, bail her to appear on the 15th of August, to which he very cheerfully acceded. The woman went home after having promised that she would never again drink intoxicating liquor. This was on Friday, and the lady who had first interested herself, was present at the interview. On Sunday following, I called upon the woman whom I had bailed, and the interview was indeed a happy one; the children were neatly dressed, and were about to start for the Sabbath school, and the very atmosphere was redolent with peace and happiness; although so short a time had elapsed, the mother appeared like a very different woman; she had signed the pledge and most sacredly she kept it. She appeared in court at the specified time, and was fined one cent and costs. She afterwards became *a devoted* member of the Martha Washington Temperance Society. Some time during the next year, there was a tea party at Tremont Temple, the originators of which was the Martha Washington Society. Dr. Channing was present, and during the evening I heard him address a lady of the name of her whom I had bailed the year before, and I found it to be no other than her, and was assured that she was one of the most efficient members of that excellent society. Such an instance was to me additional evidence of the efficacy and humanity of my plan.

I have now related in an unvarnished manner the occasions on which I bailed the first man and first woman, and I need not therefore particularize cases which since have become more than a thousand. That year I bailed forty-six persons, of which number four were females, and thirty I have every reason to believe, abandoned the vice which brought them to the prisoner's bench; but a small proportion of the number were too strongly wedded to a career of guilt and were incorrigible.

During the year ending December 31, 1842, the amount of my bail bonds were $1,380, and the amount of fines paid $174.86.

During the year 1843, I bailed a number of persons who were charged with various offences, my efforts hitherto having been exclusively for the benefit of the drunkard. In the latter part of this year, I bailed two little girls, aged eight and ten years, and one little boy aged eleven. The girls were sisters. These children had been indicted at the October term, and of course their cases were entered on the docket of the Municipal Court. The girls were charged with stealing five or six dollars from a grocery store on Washington street.— These girls sold apples, and entered the store daily to offer their fruit for sale, and at such times those employed in the store would often teaze them by playfully seizing their apples. This familiarity of course, caused the children to be pert and to act in a similar manner with the property of the grocer, and on one occasion one of them took a small sum of money from a drawer; they shared it equally, and were soon after arrested for larceny from a shop and confined in jail. The next day they were brought before the Police Court for examination. The father of the little ones was present and was allowed to speak for them if he desired, but he was evidently intoxicated; he spoke in a very unfeeling manner of the elder child, saying that "she was to blame, and might go to jail, it was good enough for her," but spoke in a different manner of the other. The Justice ordered them both to find surety each in the sum of $100, and for default to be committed to jail. I offered myself as surety for the little one and was accepted. I took the child to my house, and placed her in charge of my wife; the other went to jail. The next day I went in quest of her mother, and after some difficulty found her, but in a state of intoxication, and of course unable to converse about her children. It was not a fit place for these little ones, neither were those whom nature intended as their guardians, at all competent to take proper care of them. A few days after I had witnessed this melancholy sight, a humane gentleman, Mr. H., called on me, and expressed his desire to take the little girl who was then in jail, into his own family. I offered to bail her, and immediately proceeded to the Police Court, for that purpose, and was at once accepted as her surety. We proceeded directly to the jail, where we found the little one crying bitterly. The iron door swung creaking on its hinges, to allow of the egress of the little prisoner. I took her tiny hand in mine and led her from the place, while the child looked up into my face, and there beamed from her eyes an expression I can never forget. Who would know true joy, let him be a participant in a scene like this. I could fancy a language proceeding from that gaping cell which was now untenanted; it said in unmistakable language, "Take this infant under thy guardian care, for she has none to help her; be thou her father and her guide, then shall the blessings of those that are ready to perish come upon you. Say to her, remember this day in which you came from out the prison of bondage, for by strength of hand the Lord has brought thee out of this place."

My friend took the little one to the bosom of his own family, and the sequel is soon told;—they both became good girls, and were brought up aright; the elder one is now married happily, and resides in Worcester county of this State.

At the expiration of this year, (1843,) upon looking over my records, I found that I had bailed fifty-three persons at the Police Court, and four in the Municipal Court. The amount of my bail bonds in the Municipal Court was $520, in the Police Court, $1,694. I have related the above instance to show the reason of my carrying my labors into the Municipal Court. Another reason for my operating in this court was that perhaps one person in ten whom I bailed for drunkenness, for various reasons did not appear at the assigned time, and of course the cases of such were defaulted. It has been a rule of the court that the defendant must subsequently appear within a specified time—ten days, or the default could not be taken off, and therefore the bonds were forfeited; occasionally defendants were sick, others absent, some perhaps forgot the time at which they were to appear, and occasionally some would be drunk, and of course unable to appear, and whenever such cases did occur, the papers were sent up to the County Attorney; it was necessary for him to sue me, which he did in cases of common drunkards. This course was necessary as a legal form, but the Judges always remitted the penalty, as such accidents are occasionally unavoidable; and from business of this character and being summoned, I found my way to the Municipal Court. Here I regret to say that I met with much opposition from the officers when they discovered the nature of my labors, but that unfriendly spirit if as rife, was not so frequently and so visibly manifested, as at the Police Court, for here I had the protection of the Judges and the Sheriff, whom I found were by no means unfavorable to my efforts. When I first attempted to enter this court, I occasionally observed the same officers lurking about, whom I had occasion to remember in the Police Court, and they were evidently alarmed at the progress I was making.

At this time I was constantly bailing some one in the Police Court to appear here for trial. Often when I attempted to enter the court room, I was rudely repulsed by the officers and told that I could not go in, as their orders were imperative to admit no one except members of the bar; on one occasion of this kind, having particular business in the court room, I informed the officer of the fact, (of which however he was previously aware) but he replied as before; I immediately addressed a note to the sheriff, which I transmitted by a member of the bar, and was at once, after this system of telegraphing, admitted. When I returned I was crowded back and not allowed a seat where the members of the bar sat, even though there were at the time a number of unoccupied chairs, but I contented myself with the thought that I was fast gaining ground. I subsequently took a seat, but was soon rudely expelled without the least cause. I would always obey, but generally returned to my seat, although I received a reprimand of the petty officials who "clothed with a little brief authority," took inconceivable delight in thus causing me inconvenience. I always endeavored to keep myself as cool and as calm as possible under such treatment, keeping my object constantly in view. By being driven back I was not unfrequently brought in contiguity with the prisoner's dock, so that I could easily converse with the prisoners, and this was the very object I desired; but when they discovered this act on my part, the duties of their office required them to prohibit such conversation.

Here then, were two points gained,—to take my place with the members of the bar, and to occasionally whisper a word of hope to the desponding heart of some unfortunate and perhaps innocent person. This opposition was not unexpected or singular, for my conduct was new to them; no one had ever before attempted to aid or befriend the prisoner in this way in this court. I soon found ample occasion to address the judge, and at such times was always listened to with as much attention as was any member of the bar,—this was the greatest point yet attained, for I received that attention which I craved, and on no occasion was I ever treated otherwise than any one should be who was engaged in a work like mine.

I became considerably acquainted with the prisoners, their offences, their wants and condition, and occasionally found those arraigned who had little cause to hope for justice by reason of their poverty and ignorance, in opposition to the power, experience and learning of the prosecuting attorney. Often I would find a very youthful prisoner, who was arraigned for the first time in his life, and who was never before within the walls of a court house; destitute of friends to advise, or money to procure counsel, which means, if within their power, might perhaps, establish the proof of their innocence.

A woman perhaps, is charged with stealing an article; she is innocent. and pleads 'not guilty,'—she is put upon trial, the evidence is strong against her, and it may be purely circumstantial,—she has no counsel, yet she is told by the court that she can ask the witness any questions,—but she dares not interrogate him; she is told that if she desires she can address the jury; here she appears abashed and bewildered, and *cannot* say a word in explanation of the act. The jury retire, and subsequently bring in a verdict of guilty, when, had she any legal adviser to assist, she might have established her innocence and been spared the infamy and punishment for the commission of a crime, which she would never have committed. There are many prisoners whose cases are thus disposed of, and who receive no justice.

Here then, was opportunity for me to labor, for I thought it as much a duty to have the temple of justice watched, and to inquire who are imprisoned that should go free, to investigate the merits of cases and to allow the innocent opportunity to show their innocence, as for the accuser to attempt to show their guilt.

If my observations have been correct, I have found that wrong customs prevail sometimes in courts of justice as well as in communities, and that the minds of the dispensers of justice may occasionally be biased in favor or against a prisoner, by the external circumstances by which he may be surrounded; in view of that state of things I resolved to bail some of the pitiable objects whenever prudence might dictate. At first I was inclined to shrink from so doing, as I was surety for a number in the Police Court, and was constantly taking upon myself other and like responsibilities, but I offered myself as bail, and was readily accepted by the court. This course opened the door for numerous applications to me to aid others in a similar manner, and I offered myself again and again, and always with approval. It should not be supposed that I assumed such obligations merely at the solicitation of the unfortunate, or without due investigation into the merits of their cases and a scrupulous examination into the history and character of each individual.

I continued this course for a time, when on one occasion, Mr. S. D. Parker, the county attorney, objected to my becoming surety, stating to the court as the ground of his objection, that I was not competent in regard to property; this objection was properly made, as he had an eye single to the interests of the State treasury, and in this was but performing his duty. I was aware of the force of his objection, but the case in hand was one of especial interest and importance; it was that of a woman who had been indicted for keeping a house of ill-fame, but who had given assurances that if I would become surety for her, she would abandon her course of life, and would return to her friends in the country; I stated the case to the court and requested to be allowed to assume the bonds; his Honor overruled all objection, and I was again accepted. The woman performed all that she had promised, and I have reason to believe abandoned her guilty career. My object was accomplished, and subsequently, by consent of the court, and of Mr. Parker, 1 was allowed to bail others, when by so doing the object of the law would be accomplished, and there appeared an intention to reform, in the party charged with the offence.

That year I had a great amount of labor to perform, and the character of my duties had become various. I was now obliged to bestow a share of my time and attention upon both courts, to bail large numbers of persons and to bear their cases in mind, to keep their numbers correctly, to watch the calling of the court docket, to see if the assigned cases in the police court were called up at the specified times, and lastly, but not least, in contending with the opposition that I was compelled to encounter. I made up my mind that the spirit of the opposition sprung from envy, hatred, ill-will and strife, and must therefore, be overcome with good. I had marked well the shoals and rocks, and could guide my bark successfully and in tolerable safety over this somewhat dangerous sea.

I found that the reason for opposition in the Municipal Court was similar to that in the *court below ;* their fees for serving a mittimus to jail, were sixty-two cents, and every person whom I bailed required no mittimus, and thus of course, in such cases there was no opportunity for earning the fee.

It became pretty generally known that my labors were upon the ground of reform, that I confined my efforts mainly to those who were indicted for their first offence, and whose hearts were not wholly depraved, but gave promise of better things ; it was also known that I received no compensation for so doing, and it early appeared that the judges were favorably disposed toward my plan of operation. That year I bailed one hundred and forty-eight persons, one hundred and ten of whom were in the Police Court, and the remainder in the Municipal Court; of this number forty-five were women and girls.

I need not weary the patience of my friends by a detailed account of the proceedings in this court or in the mention of the too frequent scenes of opposition. My path was strewed with obstacles which required both patience and perseverance to remove.

As illustrative of some of the lesser obstacles which I was sometimes called upon to overcome, I will extract a brief notice from the *Morning Post,* which was published about the time I first began my labors in the Municipal Court.

"Ann —— was called for sentence, convicted of petty larceny, which brought Mr. John Augustus to his feet, and the following is the substance of what occurred:

Mr. Augustus. I thought your Honor, that Ann was not to be sentenced till next term ?

Mr. Parker—(county attorney). Why not? I know no reason why she should not be sentenced now; nothing has been said to me about postponing it.

Mr. Augustus. Yes there has. I said something about it myself—and I understood his Honor that the sentence was put off.

Mr. Parker. You may have expressed yourself to that effect, but not in my presence. Perhaps the gentleman will seat himself on the *Bench* sometime!

Mr. Augustus. Perhaps I shall, (a laugh)—or *under* the bench. I'll try to speak so as to be understood. Ann's mother is away now out of the city and the girl is in a good place, out of the way of bad example; and I think we shall be able to make a reformed woman of her—if your Honor will give us time. What's the use of being in a hurry to punish the girl when kindness may save her?

Mr. Parker.—We do not wish to punish, except for a purpose of warning others. I will not urge a sentence now, if it interferes with any plan for the reformation of the girl; but that cannot be brought about by sending her to her mother.

Mr. Augustus.—We do not propose to send Ann to her mother; I think myself it would do her no good. She is but sixteen years old, and she possesses a good heart, amiable and kind feelings, and though she has been guilty of stealing some small articles, yet she is too young to be very wicked; and I am confident that if she can remain in the excellent place where she is now, for a time, she will be a good girl hereafter. I am her bail and I want your Honor to postpone her sentence till next term (and I thought it was so understood) to give us an opportunity of saving her—leading her in a new course, and making her live a better life—which I believe can be done.

His Honor listened attentively to the remarks of the worthy philanthropist, and granted the request."

In 1845, I continued my labors in both courts as in former years. In the early part of this year, a woman was indicted for keeping a house of ill-fame in the south part of the city; her perlieu of vice was in one of our fashionable streets, and was a constant source of annoyance to the citizens in the neighborhood, and at length she was called to answer for the violation of the law. She was required to give bail for her appearance for trial, and importuned me to become her surety, giving me her promise that if I would do so, she would leave the city, abandon her career of vice, and return to her friends in the State of New York. I thought her removal from the city would not cause much grief, or her absence prove detrimental to the morals of that part of the city, and having confidence in her promise, I bailed her, and in a fortnight she removed to S., in the State of New York, the home of her friends. As the court was not in session at that time, of course the case could not be disposed of. I had informed her that the law allowed the Judge to impose a small fine for a first offence, and that this course had generally been pursued, and thus obtained her promise to return to Boston at such time as her case might be called for trial. At the opening of the next term, I requested a continuance of the case till another term, which was granted. I wrote to the woman, advising her of the assigned time, and stated that the case could probably be settled for *thirty* dollars. She came back to this city, but unfortunately I was absent. She applied to a lawyer, and was in high hopes of having the matter settled on the following day. The next morning I went into court, intending to pay the fine, but was informed that the defendant must be present, and unfortunately I had forgotten her place of temporary residence, nor did her counsel remember; here then was a dilemma; the woman was ignorant of the requirement and I ignorant of her whereabouts, and of course I was defaulted. The woman learned the fact, and being informed that she would be sent to the House of Correction, she became alarmed and immediately returned to New York without seeing me.

The County Attorney sued me forthwith, and Sheriff Eveleth called upon me and said that his duty was to attach my goods and chattels, if he could find any, and if not to take my body, and it (my body) must in that case be kept safe, so that no one else could take it, before the next term of the Municipal Court; at that time it would probably be made to appear that I had designedly committed a violation of the law. I recollected that I had caused one house in Shawmut to become desolate, and there was but one other house upon that street, similar in character to the one now deserted.

I asked how much time would be allowed me to find security, and was informed until three o'clock of that day. I complied with his demands, placed two hundred dollars in his hands, and was permitted to enjoy my liberty, and to continue my labors, from the prosecution of which I was by no means discouraged. I did not run away, but made my appearance every day during the session of the Court for the next term, and continued my efforts as before. That term the noble hearted Judge, Luther S. Cushing, presided. When my case was called, I pleaded guilty to the forfeiture of the bond, but asked a remission of the penalty. One half of the sum paid was immediately remitted; so that I had actually paid one hundred dollars for breaking up a den of vice, and making an effort to reform the abandoned, by which in various ways, I had saved the county and the Commonwealth at least two or three thousand dollars, to say nothing of the removal of bad influences. I then became aware that it was useless to attempt to break up a den of vice of this kind, as the strong arm of the law was averse to such an act.

I was advised to petition the Legislature for a remission of the money paid, and I determined to appeal to the State's paternal ear. Judge Cushing signed a petition to this effect, and stated that from a careful investigation into the circumstances of the case, I ought to receive back the money. The petition was referred to a Committee of the Legislature.

I went before the Committee and made a full statement of the case; I explained to them that I was instrumental in saving the Commonwealth a large sum annually, and also stated my relation to the unfortunate, but those men after much deliberation, decided that the ends of justice had been thwarted, and that the petition should not be granted; they thought justice could only be answered by sending such persons to the House of Correction for punishment, and this I had prevented. That Committee perhaps were not aware of the fact that al-

most invariably all who are sent to the House of Correction,
for such offences, at the expiration of their term of imprisonment, return to their former mode of life; there may be instances where such is not the case, but I know of none.

According to the decision of this Committee, punishment
must be administered upon those who abandon their course of
vice as upon those who do not. The object of the law is to
reform criminals, and to prevent crime and not to punish maliciously, or from a spirit of revenge. Acting upon that principle which actuated the Committee in the case before them,
what would they do if the keepers of every den of vice in Boston, upon being indicted, should forfeit their bonds by removing into the country, and becoming good members of society?
It was to effect this object as far as possible,—the removal of
such persons from the city, that I adopted the course which I
did, and I think if any money should have been paid at all,
the operation should have been reversed and the money paid
to those who labored to accomplish the end of the law, and
the benefit of society; I think the reader will admit that such
a course would have been more in accordance with justice.

Would it not be more in consonance with the desires of the
thinking part of society, and more productive of good, to allow
such persons and those who sell spirituous liquors to be bailed,
on a plea of guilty, on the ground of their renouncing their
business, and to discharge the bail by laying the indictment
on file when such places shall have been thus broken up?
Such a course would be perfectly safe, for if the party should
again be guilty of a violation of the law, the indictment can
be taken from file, and upon it the party can be brought in
for sentence; with this indictment hanging over them, there is
little danger of a new offence of similar character. Of course
this rule would not be applicable to the cases of those indicted as common thieves, robbers, or for the commission of
many other kinds of felony, but may safely be used in the
cases above mentioned. But enough upon this point.

During the year I bailed a number of young females, who
were destitute of a home, and for whom I was obliged to find

a temporary abode; I had so many calls of this kind, that I was brought in contact with all sorts of people, and every grade of society, and thus my labors became extremely arduous. I was frequently obliged to incur the expense of carriage hire, and as a matter of economy and convenience, I resolved to adopt a new mode of traveling, and therefore bought a horse and chaise. I employed him a large portion of every day; I have used the same animal to the present time, and he appears to be pretty familiar with every part of the city; the Jail and the Court House have been his usual stopping places; one chaise after another has done excellent service, and become worthless; three have already been worn out, and the fourth is now in requisition. I have traveled 15,000 miles within the limits of the city; 4,000 women have been conveyed in my carriages to and from various parts of the city.

That year I made 1,500 calls and received more than this number at my house. I bailed in both courts, one hundred and thirty-three, forty-five of whom were females. The amount of my bonds was $13,020.

It became evident that an Asylum should be established for the drunkard, and the following Memorial was presented to the Legislature:

GENTLEMEN,—The undersigned, inhabitants of the County of Norfolk, have noticed with great satisfaction, that an order has been submitted to the House of Representatives, by one of its members, Mr. Charles Wade, of the city of Boston, in relation to the founding of an Asylum for the temporary abode of that large class of misguided persons who so frequently render themselves obnoxious to the laws by the vice of intemperance.

It would be the desire of your petitioners to present the true condition of the unfortunate class referred to, with much greater particularity than is usual in the customary form of a petition. *The subject calls for a Memorial.* It is believed that the present method provided by law for the guardianship and punishment of victims of intemperance, imperatively calls for investigation. It is believed that the largest portion of this class, who are, according to our present laws, now locked up in Jails and Houses of Correction, and lost to their families, to society, and to themselves, may be restored to usefulness and respectability, by the establishment of a State Asylum, expressly devoted to their cure.

In order, gentlemen, to bring the subject into closer view, your petitioners invite your attention to a few facts.

Early in the year 1841, a society now known as the Parent Washington Total Abstinence Society, was formed in the city of Boston. Large numbers of persons, in various stages of intoxication and destitution, who have been found in the streets and elsewhere, have been led to Washingtonian Hall, where they have been kindly received, and their necessary wants supplied. The amount of service which has been rendered within the last four years, by this society, cannot be readily apprehended. A multitude of men who, by intemperance, had been shut out from the friendly regard of the world, found in the hall of the Washingtonians, for the time being, a comfortable asylum; and these men departed thence to resume their position as useful citizens. About 750 of such persons have found a temporary home at Washingtonian Hall, during the year just closed, nearly all of whom, it is believed, are now temperate and industrious members of society. The expenses of this establishment have fallen principally upon the members of the Parent Society, many of whom are poor men, and have little to spare from their earnings, but who contribute their utmost to sustain an humble asylum, within whose walls are put into operation the Samaritan principles which caused their own reform. Much of their valuable time, too, do these men give to this noble work, without the slightest pecuniary reward; and their devoted secretary, all of whose time is given to this great reform, has received but an insignificant sum for his untiring and invaluable services. The managers of this establishment have, under God, saved the lives of many of their fellow-men. They have restored to their families a very large number of grateful human beings, who, but for their philanthropic efforts, would now, without doubt, be wanderers and vagabonds on the earth, or occupants of the House of Correction.

In the summer of 1841, JOHN AUGUSTUS, a man in humble life, now well known to the friends of temperance in Boston, and who deserves to be throughout the State, visited the Police Court in Boston, and, being very much interested in the case of a poor man, who, for the vice of drunkenness, had been sentenced to the House of Correction, stepped forward and offered to become bail for him. His proposal was accepted. He paid, out of his own pocket, the fees of court, amounting to a few dollars, and took the condemned man with him out of the court room. He persuaded him to sign the pledge, furnished him with food and lodgings, and at last secured employment for him, and from henceforth the rescued drunkard became an industrious and sober citizen.

Mr. Augustus, inspired by the success of his first attempt, and impelled by the yearnings of his noble heart, continued his visits to the Police Court, and from August, in the year 1841, to February of the present year, has rescued from the jaws of the House of Correction and from the fellowship of convicted felons, one hundred and seventy-six men and fifty-six women,—in all, *two hundred and thirty-two human beings,* —a large portion of whom, but for the vice of intemperance, would have enjoyed an unquestionable right to the general regard of society. Fortunately for this benevolent attempt to stand between the drunkard and the customary course of law, Mr. Augustus has preserved a careful record of every case in which he has interested himself, and he is thus enabled to furnish an intelligent account of a large portion of the persons who, by his means, have been saved from confinement in South Boston. Full three-fourths of the number, are now temperate and orderly citizens, and are gaining a respectable livelihood. About one half of the whole number were residents of Boston, and the other half were temporary visitors to the city from the country and from neighboring States. The proportion of foreigners was much larger of the men than the women. The amount of costs paid by Mr. Augustus, for the release of these persons, is $976 61. This amount has nearly all been paid back to him by the persons thus rescued. Of course, this amount of costs has been saved to the towns liable for it. It will be readily seen, however, that a much larger sum has been saved, by so many intemperate persons having become useful citizens, instead of being shut up in prison at the public charge. To those towns in the country which occasionally receive large bills for the support of drunkards in the House of Correction in South Boston, this point is not unworthy of notice. These considerations are glanced at, because, indeed, they should not be overlooked; but they are of little moment in comparison with the tears which have been dried up, the hearts which have been healed, and the families which have been made happy, by the restoration of so large a number of the great human brotherhood, to temperance, usefulness and respectability. By the minute and unquestionable records kept by Mr. Augustus, rising eight-tenths of all the persons sent to the House of Correction are sent there for drunkenness, or offences occasioned by drunkenness. Through his Samaritan efforts, the number of commitments for this dreadful vice has been largely reduced,—and besides the diminished expense, consequent upon such reduction, the community has been incalculably blessed by the change.

The following statement will show the actual reduction in the commitments, to the House of Correction, for Drunkenness, since the Washingtonian reform commenced in Boston, but, especially, as resulting from the efforts of Mr. Augustus. In 1841, they were 605; in 1842, they were 541; in 1843, 456; in 1844, 407. On the 1st of January, of the present year, the number of persons remaining in the House of Correction, committed by the Police Court, was only 123; of which number 110 were committed for drunkenness, viz.: 47 males and 63 females, all other offences being but 13. During the first year, Mr. Augustus has saved 120 persons from the House of Correction; 20 of whom have since been sentenced to the House of Correction, the remaining 100 are doing well. It would be easy to show the actual amount, in dollars and cents, saved to the State, by a result like this; but not as easy to exhibit the blessings resulting to the rescued men, or to their families, many of the members of which would, doubtless, otherwise have become outcasts, or have found their way to our alms-houses.

It is impossible to enter, in detail, into the formidable difficulties which a humble mechanic, like Mr. Augustus, has had to encounter, in order to proceed in his beneficent work. To say nothing of the formalities and liabilities which belong, alike, to all courts of law, he has, in most cases, provided a temporary home for his fallen brother, and allowed no rest to his head, until he has done his utmost to procure for him employment. It should be added that, within a few months, a number of the "merchant princes," and other eminent philanthropists, of Boston, have given Mr. Augustus a substantial testimonial of their respect for his unwearied and invaluable services. Previous to this liberal act, Mr. A. had relied upon his own scanty resources, and had found it exceedingly difficult to carry into effect his praiseworthy labors.

The labors of the managers of Washingtonian Hall, and of John Augustus, have been brought into distinct review, because they present a concentration of facts, of remarkable import. They exhibit, it is believed, the great benefit which, in a humble way, has been conferred on society, by rescuing from disgrace, and from destruction, so many members of the human family. They start the inquiry, that, if so important a service to fallen humanity can be brought about with so imperfect arrangements, and with so limited means, cannot a yet more important work be accomplished by the establishment of an Asylum, calculated to carry out, with more completeness, and with far greater advantages, the objects which have been partially obtained under such great and obvious disadvantages?

Your petitioners believe that greater and more efficient than all other instrumentalities hitherto employed, for saving the drunkard, *is the law of kindness.* It having been demonstrated of late, in thousands of cases, that the drunkard is yet a man, and can be restored to health by kind words and kind deeds, ought he not to be placed in the most favorable position for his recovery? Has not the word gone forth in Massachusetts, never to be again recalled, that the poor maniac shall no longer shiver in his cage, without clothing, and without fire,— that his chains shall be stricken off, and that he shall henceforth find comfort, and, perhaps, restored reason, in a State Asylum? And what is the drunkard, with his periodical fits of delirium tremens, *but* a maniac? A shattered mind can be healed only by skillful words, uttered in tones of kindness; by efficient medicines, administered by persuasion, and not by force.

Gentlemen, we hope that none of you may ever have the misfortune to have a beloved brother a houseless wanderer, by the curse of intemperance; we hope you may be spared the sorrow, in your old age, of hearing that the son of your own blood, who, in the confidence of your hearts, you have sent to the capital of the State to acquire consideration and wealth, in mercantile or other honorable pursuits, has " fallen among thieves," and perished in the dark lanes or darker dens of the city, before the good Samaritan has searched him out and placed him where a father's love can reach him and save him ! We hope, gentlemen, *you* may be spared this terrible calamity;—but if, in the inscrutable dealings of Providence, a child of your affections should be cast forth in destitution by reason of the intoxicating cup, we trust in your wisdom, you will, with the responsibilities of your high duties pressing upon you, see *now*, if such an Asylum exists as the unhappy wanderer requires, which the age demands, and which your noble State, in every other great work of Christian charity is amply provided with.

We have not written out the appeal of the wretched drunkard himself, who, with feeble body and broken spirit, entreats you not to send him to a charnel house of living corruption ! but to give him a Christian resting place, where he can put forth all his strength to burst the bands which have bound him; and instead of going forth from its threshold with the mark of the prison branded upon him, that he may depart with the strong courage which gratitude gives, and with thanksgivings to God that he has been restored to his right mind by the strong arm of a brother's faith, and the warm breath of a brother's love !

The only object they have had in view was to call the attention of the Legislature to a subject of great magnitude in its bearings, inasmuch as it is closely connected with our present pauper and prison discipline, and relates to the well being of at least three-fourths of those who now crowd our prisons and almshouses.

In the countless number of noble institutions which have risen up around us; in the constant exhibition of munificent charities which are daily announced to us, a testimony has been recorded, that the beautiful spirit of Christian benevolence is an active principle in our midst. And in presenting some of the reasons for founding a State Asylum for the relief and restoration of the victim of intemperance, your petitioners hope that the object will be considered worthy of the careful consideration of the Legislature, and that the growing tendencies in behalf of suffering humanity, may result in a substantial effort for the benefit of the poor drunkard!

Respectfully submitted,

EDGAR K. WHITAKER,

And fifty others.

February 17, 1845.

This petition called forth the following REPORT :

Your Committee met the petitioners at several times, and listened with much interest to such statements and evidence as they were desirous to present.

It appeared that, of all the commitments to the House of Correction, in the county of Suffolk, much the largest number had been for the offences of drunkenness and being common drunkards; that, of the persons so committed, nearly all were sentenced more than once, some as many as fifteen or twenty times, and giving an average of at least five sentences to each of these victims of intemperance; and that frequently but a few days would pass between the discharge and the return of the offenders. This showed conclusively that the imprisonment had a very slight tendency to produce the reformation of those who are its subjects; and that, unless some other remedy were found, a man or woman, once sentenced to imprisonment, for an offence of this kind, would, in all probability, continue to require and receive similar punishment indefinitely thereafter.

Such a state of things impressed so strongly the mind of Mr. John Augustus, a worthy citizen of Boston, that happening, in the winter of 1841-2, to be in court when a man was found guilty as a common drunkard, he determined to try the experiment whether something could not be done to save him from destruction.

It was the success which attended this benevolent and persevering effort, which suggested the application made by the petitioners.

At the hearings, it was found that the views and wishes of the petitioners were not wholly identical, nor limited at all to what the petition itself had expressed. The petition itself prayed for the establishment of a *temporary home* for poor drunkards, either upon their discharge from the House of Correction, or when found houseless and friendless, not having been sentenced to confinement. Some of the petitioners wished to extend the plan to a large institution in the nature of a hospital, to which inebriates of all sorts might be sent for safety and reformation, somewhat analagous to the State institution for the insane. Others desired the State to furnish a house of refuge, in which might be accommodated temporarily the persons for whom any individual should become bail, and to provide for their support until they could procure employment; and still another plan, and the one upon which the petitioners finally united as the most practicable and important, was, to do away the necessity for giving bail in such cases altogether, by providing for the appointment of an agent, who should be furnished with means to procure and support an asylum at the expense of the Commonwealth, and authorizing the courts, in their discretion, to commit to his charge persons convicted as common drunkards or for drunkenness, for the purpose of attempting their reformation.

Upon mature deliberation and reflection, however, your Committee were unable to find, in either of the plans presented, what seemed to them a proper basis for legislation on the part of the Commonwealth. To the worth and importance of the objects which the petitioners are striving to promote, it can hardly be necessary for them to bear testimony. A roll was exhibited to the Committee, containing the names and places of residence of the three hundred men and women who had been saved by the untiring and disinterested philanthropy of Mr. Augustus, in the manner above described, with the date of the conviction, the time to which sentence was deferred, and the sum finally paid in each case; and it was impossible to look without emotion upon such a record of the unpretending but noble labors of a single man in the cause of humanity and virtue. Among the names of the benefactors of their race, few deserve a higher place than that of JOHN AUGUSTUS; and in the day when God shall judge men "according to the deeds done in the body," when "they that turn many to righteousness shall shine as the stars forever and ever," that record will confer upon it an honor more enduring than attaches to many of the proudest achievements of statesmen or warriors.

But so many objections present themselves to the minds of the Committee against any attempt by the State to participate in this scheme of benevolence, that they have come unanimously to the conclusion, that any legislation in conformity with the prayer of the petitioners, would be inexpedient. The whole subject is one which, so far as it goes beyond the provision required by law of towns and cities for the relief of the poor and unfortunate, falls properly within the province of private charity. They have been gratified to learn that the magistrates have been disposed, to the extent of their powers, to encourage and promote the efforts of Mr. Augustus. In the belief that this encouragement will still be extended, and commending the objects of the petitioners to the enlightened liberality of the city of Boston, and to the munificence for which its citizens have always been distinguished in all humane and charitable enterprises, the Committee recommend that the petitioners have *leave to withdraw their petition.*

On behalf of the Committee,

E. ROCKWOOD HOAR, *Chairman.*

During the year 1846 I became bail to the amount of about $3000, in the Police Court, having bailed between sixty and seventy persons. That year I became surety for eleven boys, who were arrested for larceny; they were young, being from nine to thirteen years old. I also bailed ten other boys, from thirteen to sixteen years of age, and also nine girls, from fourteen to eighteen years old, who were arraigned for various offences, chiefly for larceny. By a decision of the Court upon my motion, the cases of these children were to be continued, but the question of the term of continuance caused considerable discussion. I always urged a protracted continuance, but Mr. Parker was extremely anxious to have the cases disposed of as early as possible. I wished ample time to test the promises of these youth to behave well in future. Judge Cushing was disposed to allow such cases to stand continued from term to term, and if at the expiration of a certain period, a good report was given of their behavior during the time they had been on probation, their sentences were very light.

This year my labor was extremely arduous, and every moment of my time was occupied. In addition to the calls upon my attention at court, and in procuring suitable places of employment for the females whom I bailed, a new avenue seemed to be opened; a great many females, young and old, whom I had not seen at court, called upon me to ask assistance in some form or other. Of this class I was called upon, and provided temporary homes for forty females during the year. The whole number of persons bailed in both courts was one hundred and forty-four.

The girls whom I bailed were with one exception, all discharged at the expiration of their term of probation, by the payment of a nominal fine; the girl who was not discharged, was sentenced to the House of Correction. The boys were all discharged in the same way.

In 1847, I bailed nineteen boys, from seven to fifteen years of age, and in bailing them it was understood, and agreed by the court, that their cases should be continued from term to term for several months, as a season of probation; thus each month at the calling of the docket, I would appear in court, make my report, and thus the cases would pass on for five or six months. At the expiration of this term, twelve of the boys were brought into court at one time, and the scene formed a striking and highly pleasing contrast with their appearance when first arraigned. The judge expressed much pleasure as well as surprise, at their appearance, and remarked, that the object of the law had been accomplished, and expressed his cordial approval of my plan to save and reform. Seven of the number were too poor to pay a fine, although the court fixed the amount at *ten cents* each, and of course I paid it for them; the parents of the other boys were able to pay the cost, and thus the penalty of the law was answered. The sequel thus far shows, that not one of this number has proved false to the promises of reform they made while on probation. This incident proved conclusively, that this class of boys could be saved from crime and punishment, by the plan which I had marked out, and this was admitted by the judges in both courts.

Great care was observed of course, to ascertain whether the prisoners were promising subjects for probation, and to this end it was necessary to take into consideration the previous character of the person, his age and the influences by which he would in future be likely to be surrounded, and although these points were not rigidly adhered to, still they were the circumstances which usually determined my action. In such cases of probation it was agreed on my part, that I would note their general conduct, see that they were sent to school or supplied with some honest employment, and that I should make an impartial report to the court, whenever they should desire it. This course adopted by the court I hailed as one extremely favorable to the success of my efforts, and I soon found, that it spared me an immense amount of labor which I should otherwise have been compelled to perform; I was pleased too, to observe that the opposition on the part of the District Attorney was gradually and rapidly giving way. But the toil thus saved was required in another manner, for I had frequent occasion to provide indigent girls with suitable places, and often young females were brought to my house, sometimes late at night, who required a shelter, and frequently these cases were extremely urgent; although by no means situated in a manner suited to open an asylum of this kind, I accommodated them as well as my humble means would allow. That year I took seven young girls from houses of ill-fame; these girls were from ten to thirteen years of age, the most of whom had been placed there by applications at *intelligence* offices. For these children I was obliged to incur considerable expense, in providing them with a temporary home. Sometimes young girls were brought to my house by express-men and cab-men, who felt a kind interest in their welfare.

Not unfrequently women were brought to my house by the night-watch, for very often respectable women and girls would apply to the watch-house for lodging, and in some cases, the officers very humanely referred them to my house, in the belief that I would procure them a respectable home, and proper employment. Mr. Whitwell, the captain of the west watch, who is a kind-hearted as well as very efficient officer, has himself brought females to my house, from such benevolent motives. Captain Harrington and Captain Smith, the present officers of the Municipal Court, have often done the same thing. On one occasion, Captain W. brought to my house a girl about fourteen years of age, who said that her father was drunk the night previous, and had turned her out of doors, and she was afraid to go home; her father had just been discharged from the House of Correction, and was going to beat her for having testified against him in the Police Court, at the time he was sentenced for drunkenness, although she was compelled to do so, by the requirements of the court. This girl found a home in my family for several weeks. Her father is now a reformed man and holds a responsible office in this state; she is married to a very respectable business man of this city. That year I provided temporary homes for eighty-two women and girls; and here I felt the importance of having an institution where such persons could find a home for short periods of time. This year, besides the number above mentioned, 1 bailed fifty-one in court, thus making one hundred and thirty-three females who received my aid in various ways, all of which I accomplished with satisfaction to myself, in spite of the opposition at the Police Court, which was as great as ever. That year, I bailed one hundred and twenty-five persons.

In 1848, my attention was demanded in almost every direction. I received numerous applications to provide temporary homes for unfortunate and indigent females, who were without shelter; there was no home or asylum to which they might be conducted, and the alternative was, to obtain board for them in private families, which, even at moderate rates, amounted to a large bill of expense, although they boarded only for brief periods of time. I made my condition known to some twenty-five philanthropic persons, and explained freely to them the embarrassments under which I labored, and they cheerfully agreed to contribute various sums for the establishment of a Home, where deserving and worthy females might board, as long as the exigencies of their cases might demand.

During the year I was enabled to find suitable places for, and to return to their friends, one hundred and forty-eight, who applied to me personally, or through their friends. I bailed twenty-nine females at the Police Court that year, which was a greater number than bailed any preceding year; in the Municipal Court, I bailed twenty-eight more, making the whole number *two hundred and five* females, who received my aid, time and attention, during the year, which is on the average *four* per week for the whole time. Almost all the cases in which I stood as surety were settled without being brought to trial; and pleas of guilt being put in, a door was opened for the mercy of the court, which was frequently applied and with most salutary effect, but in some cases the parties continued to pursue their former sinful career, and the justice of the law was measured to them according to the nature of their offences.

I invariably reported to the court, a true statement of the case, to the best of my knowledge, which was the result of personal observation, and requested the court to dispose of them in a manner in which I should have done had I held the office of a judge, but of course, the opinion of the court was in many cases, different from my own.

This year I accomplished a greater amount of labor in bailing persons, than during any other single year since beginning my labors in the courts; besides the number of females for whom I assumed such responsibilities, I bailed eighty-eight men and boys, in both courts, and all cases were disposed of without any forfeiture of bail.

In the year 1849 and 1850, I frequently resolved to leave the Police Court, and confine my labors exclusively to the Municipal Court, believing I could thereby accomplish a greater amount of good; the cause of this state of feeling was the continued opposition and hostility which was evinced toward my efforts on every occasion, by the officers of the court. Every time in which I here attempted to aid the prisoner in any way, a storm burst upon my head in all its fury. Among the officers most vindictive, was one Mr. Stratton, who might have been indicted for assault and battery, so great was his rudeness and violence toward me on numerous occasions; but I regarded him more as an object of pity than of anger or of punishment. He had power to allow me access to the lock-up, and whenever I had occasion to request permission to thus enter, for the purpose of conversing for a few moments with prisoners who had been required to recognize to appear before the grand jury, he always took great delight in peremptorily refusing me. I would at times endeavor to expostulate with him. I would perhaps, tell him frankly, that the prisoner's counsel, 'Mr. B., or the mother of the prisoner had requested me to make the visit; but I would be told that I had better mind my own business, and his tone and manner would excite the attention of the clerk—another 'allied power,' who would pettishly exclaim, " Mr. Stratton, shut that door," and turning contemptuously toward me, ask, " what does Mr. Augustus want?" Mr. S. would then order me away, saying that he wished to close the doors. Mr. T. would then come to the rescue, to see that the orders of his brother officer were complied with, well knowing that if I succeeded in becoming bail for the prisoner, Stratton would lose the job of taking him to jail, the fee for which was *sixty-two* cents, the clerk would lose *twenty-five* cents, and the turnkey *forty* more, which he believed would be an unprofitable operation. The poor woman who was a prisoner, doubtless knew that some of the constables and officers of the court were temperate drinkers, and might be supposed to have written an inscription appropriate to be placed over the desks of the officers of the Police Court.

> " As you are now (temperate drinkers) so once was I,—
> As I am now (common drunkard) so you may be:
> Prepare for prison and follow me."

But I need not here say more of the corruption of this miscalled " temple of justice." No institution in the State calls louder for reform; and we are glad to see that the press are holding up its hideous deformities and evils to the public gaze,—and we have reason to hope that the time is near when this court shall receive attention, and have its evils eradicated. For the reasons above briefly alluded to, my efforts have of late been limited here. Another reason, however, that has prevented more extended effort on my part is, that a rule has recently been adopted here, that the person who offers himself as surety must subscribe and swear to certain documents respecting the amount of property which they may possess. I could not consistently comply with this requirement.

During the years 1849 and '50, there were a great number of respectable persons arrested on charges of petty offences, and oftentimes in such cases, the court had adjourned for the day, and the only alternative, therefore, was for them to remain in jail for a night, at least; and as such persons were frequently innocent, it was indeed a great hardship. There was no way to prevent this ignominy and privation other than to meet the Justice on his way to his residence, perhaps, and induce him to go to jail to take the recognizance of the prisoner. Viewing the matter in this light, we petitioned the judges of the Court of Common Pleas to appoint a commissioner, duly empowered to receive the recognizance of prisoners for their appearance at the Municipal Court. At the regular meeting of the judges, they appointed to this new office Mr. Thomas W. Phillips. A better choice could not have been made. He is in every respect a noble man—humane, prudent, and efficient. Since his appointment, the difficulty of which we have spoken has been wholly obviated.

Here I began to abate my labors in the Police Court, as I was able to accomplish an equal amount of good, without being brought in daily contact with so much that was disagreeable. In the year 1849, I bailed, in the Police Court, forty-one persons, and in the ensuing year, but twenty; but in the Municipal Court, during this period, I bailed one hundred and twenty-six persons. In 1851, I bailed *fifteen* in the Police Court, while in the Municipal Court, about six times that number. By the statistical tables on the following pages, the reader will readily see in brief, a synopsis of my labors in the courts for the ten years.

SYNOPSIS OF MY LABORS IN THE POLICE COURT.

From December 1841, to December 1851.	Whole number of Persons Bailed by me.	Males.	Females.	Amount of Bail.	Amount of Fines and Costs.	REMARKS.
1841	17	17	4	$570	$60.87	Began my labors in the Police Court.
1842	46	42	14	1,380	174.86	This year advocated "Woman's Rights."
1843	53	39	24	1,694	190.16	Found my way to the Municipal Court.
1844	110	86	25	3,300	394.91	A petition to the Legislature for an Asylum for Drunkards.
1845	77	52	25	2,310	278.29	Refused admittance to the House of Correction, on Dr. Moriarty's permit.
1846	66	41	13	2,010	253.25	
1847	44	31	29	1,320	141.58	Fainted in the Police Court—not expected to live.
1848	80	51	14	2,490	149.93	
1849	41	27	10	2,160	135.60	A Boy seven years old indicted for rape.
1850	20	10	9	600	90.90	Removal of Prisoners from the old jail.
1851	15	6		560	71.30	
For the term of ten years.	569	401	168	$18,394	$1,951.65	

SYNOPSIS OF MY LABORS IN THE

MUNICIPAL COURT.

From January 1844, to December 1851.	Whole number of Persons Bailed by me.	Males.	Females.	Amount of Bail.	Items paid by me in part for Fines and Costs.	REMARKS.
1844	38	17	21	$5,275	$33,	Bonds forfeited for $100 and paid.
1845	57	33	24	10,710	70,	
1846	78	37	41	10,515	62,	19 small boys bailed this year and discharged on good behavior.
1847	81	43	38	9,380	47,	
1848	65	37	28	9,205	42,	The amounts in the column of "fines and costs," is made up of various sums paid for different persons.
1849	68	34	34	10,150	68,	
1850	58	28	30	10,030	65,	
1851	88	44	44	15,405	79,	
For the term of eight years.	533	273	260	$81,070	$466,	
Total in Both Courts.	1102	674	428	$99,464	$2,417.65	

In the year 1849, I provided suitable places for sixty-eight females; in 1850, one hundred and one; and in 1851, seventy-three; making in all 253 persons for whom either homes or places of employment were obtained by me. Of this number many were children, from five to twelve years of age. A number of the little girls I placed under the charge of Mrs. Garnaut, the Matron of the Childrens' Home for the Destitute, No. 26 Albany street. The institution is an excellent one, and has already been of incalculable benefit. I will mention one or two circumstances which were the immediate inducements for me to endeavor to establish a Home, which, by the blessing of Heaven, is now in a flourishing and prosperous condition.

On a cold morning, late in the autumn of 1847, a gentleman called at my house and stated that, on opening his store, on Hanover street, that morning, he discovered a little girl about six years of age. The child appeared to belong to very poor parents, but who they were, or where they lived, could not be ascertained. A lady near by the shop had taken the child into her house, until I should make some disposition of it. Upon interrogating the child, I learned that she had no father or mother, but that she lived with her aunt, in Cross street. She had wandered away from the miserable home the day before, and had entered the store unperceived, and had slept beneath the counter that night. I took the child by the hand, and walked toward the spot she pointed out; but the carpenters were at that moment tearing the house down. The child's relative had removed, and though efforts were made to find her, they were in vain. I took the child to my house, where my wife provided for her for several days, and subsequently placed her in charge of a very kind lady, in Wrentham, in whose family she now lives.

While this little one was at my house, a lady found a little girl, about seven years of age, in the street, and crying bitterly. She took the child by the hand, won her confidence, and learned from her that her mother, who had been a very intemperate woman, had just dropped dead in a fit; and she now had no friend in the world to care for her. She was brought to my house, and I kept her for a few days, when I felt obliged to obtain a permit to allow her to go to the Alms House; and never did I feel so bad as when I placed the little one there: and I then resolved never again, under similar circumstances, to cause a child to be placed there, if I could possibly avoid it.

I told the story of those children to some humane persons connected with Rev. Mr. Clarke's society; and the story was not an idle tale. That year the society were contemplating the erection of a church edifice, but postponed it: they therefore resolved to establish such a Home as was thus loudly called for. A meeting was called at the residence of a member of the society, and I there presented the child from Hanover street; and the artless prattle of the child, its appearance, and its history, were the only arguments used in advocating the establishment of such an institution. A committee was soon after appointed, a suitable house hired immediately; and in January 1848, Mrs. Eliza Garnaut took the management as Matron of the Home. She continued her invaluable services in this capacity till her death, which occurred in 1849. By this bereavement society lost a worthy member, and the poor orphan a kind and loving friend. Never have I known a woman so amply qualified, both by the qualities of her heart, disposition, and habits, for the office which she held.

One day, during the year 1849, (the year in which the cholera prevailed,) as I was going toward Summer street, I met Rev. Mr. Barry, the City Missionary. He informed me that a woman lay dead in a house in Cove place, and that her infant babe was by her side. We proceeded to the spot, and discovered the babe sleeping quietly in the cold embrace of its parent. We learned from an Irish family, who occupied a part of the house, that the woman had died at twelve o'clock the night before. I carried the child to the Home at 26 Albany street; and Dr. David Thayer, of 34 Oxford street, was immediately called, and by his skillful aid, and the careful nursing of the Matron, it lived. It was two years old, and an interesting child. After it had recovered, it was given in charge of its relatives.

This excellent institution is in operation; and as no pay is ever received for supporting or providing for those who are placed there, it is supported by charity. I regret to be compelled to say, that at the present moment it requires pecuniary assistance; but I have no doubt that some humane person or society will encourage an enterprise so laudable.

For the last four or five years, I have carried two hundred females to the Temporary Home, conducted by the N. E. F. M. R. Society. It is an excellent institution; and I have no doubt by its instrumentality hundreds of girls have been saved from infamy and shame. But this society, like the one last mentioned, is greatly embarrassed for want of funds. Recently a lady in Worcester endowed it by a legacy of three thousand dollars. With this sum they have purchased and partly paid for a house, in Warren street. We sincerely hope that the humane who have the interest of unfortunate females at heart, will follow the example of Mrs. Waldo, the lady to whom we have alluded.

I have obtained more than a hundred permits for females to go to the House of Industry, and to Deer Island, and a great many others at the Massachusetts General Hospital; for these I have obtained free beds, except in one case,—in this case the free beds were all occupied, and it was not deemed possible for the applicant to live more than two or three days. I however removed her from the miserable hovel in which she was, and paid from my own pocket the fee for admission,—eighteen dollars,—and placed her under proper medical care. She lived and recovered her usual health. Often when persons have been discharged from the Hospital, I have made suitable provision for them, till they were enabled to proceed without aid.

The annexed statistical tables will no doubt prove interesting to the general reader. I have suppressed names of parties whom I have had occasion to mention,—for I have upon my records the names of more than *eight* thousand men and women, and the mention of even a few of these would create a great smoke, and some fire in our city, and could result in no benefit.

STATISTICAL TABLE,

IN REFERENCE TO EXPENSE OF COMMON DRUNKARDS SENTENCED TO THE HOUSE OF CORRECTION.

Time.	Whole number committed to the House of Correction.	Common Drunkards.	Expense for the time.	Balance after deducting Estimate of Labor.	Proportion of Expense of Common Drunkards.	For all other Offenders.	Expense of Commitments of Drunkards.
1842	668	342	$24,010.95	$13,878.47	$7,103 34	$6,775.63	$1,710
1843	643	314	19,132.79	9,061.20	4,424.26	4,636.94	1,570
1844	549	286	18,326.27	9,066.55	4,721.86	4,344 69	1,430
1845	680	393	21,445.65	11,925.27	6,889 27	5,036.36	1,965
1846	817	518	27,038.40	18,792.02	11,914.00	6,878.02	2,590
1847	823	428	29,104.62	20,804.62	10,815.56	9,989.06	2,140
1848	933	471	31,254.89	30,604.89	15,448.80	15,156.09	2,355
1849	1,164	502	32,194.92	24,700.82	10,652.44	15,054.38	2,510
1850	1,085	460	35,501.83	25,682.98	10,888.20	14,793.75	2,300
1851	1,132	454	36,607.78	20,654.78	8,280.96	12,373.82	2,270
Total.	8,494	4,168	$274,618 10	$185,171.60	$91,138.69	$94,032.91	$20,840

It will be seen by the above Table, that the proportion of expense of Common Drunkards for the whole time at the House of Correction has been $91,138 69, to which must be added the expense of making the commitments of this class of offenders, $20,840.00, which in all amounts to $111,978,69.

As my Report relative to simple drunkenness extends only from 1846 to the present, I am unable to give a statement of the expense of those who have been sentenced for simple drunkenness for the whole period : but for the term of the last six years, the cost to the Commonwealth has not been less than $21,000 : making an aggregate of expense to the State and County of $132,978.69. Nor is this all, as will be seen by the following table.

WHOLE NUMBER CONVICTED AT THE POLICE COURT,

For the last six years, for Simple and Common Drunkenness.

Time.	Number sentenced at the Police Court for Common Drunkenness.	Males.	Females.	Simple Drunkenness disposed of by payment of $2, and Costs.	Whole number of cases of Simple and Common Drunkenness.	Sentenced to the House of Correction.	Number of Common Drunkards not accounted for.
1846	737	418	319	617	1,354	518	219
1847	642	342	300	559	1,201	428	214
1848	631	334	297	719	1,350	471	160
1849	646	325	321	714	1,360	502	144
1850	721	390	331	841	1,561	460	261
1851	823	429	394	850	1,673	454	369
Total.	4,200	2,238	1,962	4,300	8,499	2,833	1,367

The above table shows that 1,367 persons have not been accounted for by the Records, yet about 600 were sent to the House of Industry, and 266 were Bailed, which reduces the number of missing to about 300.

CHAPTER II.

I CANNOT better give an idea of the details of my labors, or of the obstacles which I have had to encounter,—the thorns and the flowers which have been strewn in my pathway, than by making a few brief extracts from the newspapers, by which it will likewise appear, that others beside myself have noted the 'ups' and 'downs' I have met with in pursuance of my labors. The paragraphs which have thus appeared, have apprised the public of some few efforts of my own, but from them only, the reader could gain but an imperfect and vague idea of the immense amount of labor, the torturing anxiety, the disappointments and the pleasures that have attended my labors.

The extracts which follow are *true*, and are used for no other purpose than to convey a better idea than by any other way, the magnitude and character of my undertaking.

A SCENE IN THE BOSTON POLICE COURT.

As Reported by Wm. B. English, Esq.

The Police Court of Boston, was crowded to overflowing, for it was understood that among the creatures who had been arrested the night before, were several females, who, led away by bad examples, and an unbroken train of temptations, had at last fallen victims to remorse and the world's scorn, and become degraded outcasts of society; and upon this scene of wretchedness, hundreds came to gloat their eyes, to mock and laugh and treat with levity the sufferings of others, and to render still more bitter and polluted, the state of the unfortunate. One poor forsaken female had just been sentenced to the House of Correction, as a vagrant and abandoned one; as she stood upon the prisoner's stand, her appearance exhibited a wretchedness, want and misery, which would have excited the pity and feeling of every good man ; wretchedness, disease, scorn, had nearly driven her mad, and she appeared to feel as though the world had no communion with herself, and turning to the gaping crowd, she held her thin, bare, trembling arm on high and poured forth a curse loud and deep, upon them, while the officers hurried her away to the lock-room. This act of wild insanity on the part of the poor creature, only created mirth from the unthinking, and scarcely a single expression of sympathy was awakened in any heart for her. And what is the history of that forlorn prisoner? A few, but a few years ago, she was a beloved daughter, the joy of a happy family circle, whose presence at all times, created delightful emotions in the heart of a tender mother and a doting father. A base, a despicable villain, who lived only for the gratification of his own evil passions, saw her, and by a constant practice of his base arts, seduced her from the dear home of her parents, he poisoned the pure fountain of virtue within her breast, destroyed that holy passion ; it was a long time before that divine and early gift which her parents, through God, had planted in her heart, became destroyed ; it was long before that heart became hardened by crime, but it at length yielded to his hellish lessons and became totally corrupted, and shameless ; and the serpent guilt dwelt in the place of the pure spirit that once inhabited that beloved girl, and infusing its deadly poison into her mind, left it a prey to remorse and horror. A few years had made a sad havoc in her appearance ; that cheek now so pale and sickly, was then fresh as the morning rose, and that eye now so dull and leaden, was then full of lustre and sweetness, and that forehead now prematurely furrowed by the hand of intemperance, was once as clear and transparent as the marble, and that lip now livid with disease, lent a sweet expression to her face, which filled every beholder with rapture. This case had hardly been disposed of by the Judge, when the door of the court room was again thrown open, and another female, scarcely seventeen years of age, was conducted to the prisoner's seat; she was well dressed, but in that meretricious garb, which too plainly bespoke one of that class of poor, misguided beings, who having commenced their course of infamy, find in such a guise a fit companion of their arts. Her face was wan nd pale, and her haggard countenance contrasted strangely with her bright and sparkling dress; her hair was of a rich auburn color, and fell loosely about her neck, and a slight color tinged her cheek, while the Clerk read the charge to her. There was something in that blush and downcast look, which indicated that her deviation from the path of virtue had been recent, and that she had not yet wholly surrendered herself to the dominion of the destroyer. The life she had recently led, had stolen away much of the beauty of her person, but she was still beautiful. Poor girl, a victim of the insidious arts of a villain! She "had loved not wisely, but too well," and he had trampled upon that sacred passion, had cast her from him upon the wide world and prepared her youthful mind to receive impressions from every scene of depravity. On the brink of what an awful precipice she stood! She who had been once so constant and devoted; the gentle and confiding being, snatched like a rose from its sweet and fragrant bower, and thrown into the dust, to be trampled upon by every one, and she was known as a wanton, while she stood upon the platform allotted to prisoners. All eyes were turned towards her; the libertine, in whose eyes no principle of virtue was sacred, who regarded it only as administering to his own sensuality, gazed upon her with a smile, and made her feelings a jest for the ready ears of his comrades. There were several of these fiends in human form present, who laughed at the distress of this forlorn girl; she stood on the brink of an awful precipice! and one step more and she would be beyond the power of man to redeem! She stood friendless and alone, disowned by her parents, excluded from the society of the good, by a barrier which public opinion had thrown before her. Whichever way she turned her eye for hope, the finger of scorn was pointed at her. Poor victim of misplaced affection, betrayed and lost!

For her no tear of pity fell, no heart beat in sympathy; though that still fair brow had been dishonored she was not beyond hope. The principles of virtue had not been entirely eradicated, but within her heart there yet lingered a living spark; the rose had been crushed, it had been withered, but still lived ; the divinity within was exhibited in that flushed cheek, that moist eye, that heaving bosom, whose weight of woe nearly sunk her to the floor. She was still a precious jewel ; on the one side, the star of hope yet feebly shone, on the other, an eternity of maddening guilt, of endless horrors; it was but a step to the one or the other. Will she be saved? One by one of the constables were sworn, who severally testified to the abandoned character of the defendant, and their words were not chosen in kindness towards the unfortunate girl.

" Have you any witnesses ?" asked the Judge, of the young girl. Her reply was only in sobs and tears. " Or any thing to say to me upon the charge, and the testimony against you ?" She made no reply.

The Judge took his book and dipped his pen in ink, and was proceeding to write the dreaded sentence, by which the girl would be sent to the abode of felons, when he paused, and while his head rested on his left hand, he gazed silently in the downcast face of the girl. There was something in that tearful eye, that seemed to interest him, and it was evident that he believed that this poor girl was not far abandoned, and that he held her future destiny within his grasp. Again he dipped the pen in ink, but his mind still dwelt upon the poor creature before him, and he could not write the sentence.— That eye which sees all things on earth, directed what to do, and snatched a poor creature, overwhelmed by circumstances, like a brand from the burning. " Is any one present acquainted with the history of this defendant, or disposed to do any thing in her behalf ?"

At this moment a middle aged gentleman, who had been regarding this case with great anxiety, stepped forward and conversed with the young defendant for a few minutes, apart. He took a scrap of paper from his pocket, and sat upon the prisoners' bench by the side of her, and wrote upon the paper her name and some facts in brief, in reference to her past life. He then addressed the judge in her behalf.

"I will be her bail, your honor," said the advocate of the unfortunate betrayed one; "and what is more, I will save her." The name of this gentleman was enough, and the clerk recorded the case, as continued three weeks, and the order of the court was, that at the end of that time, if she promised reformation, the case would be dismissed. The poor girl wept, but her tears were those of joy. The noble philanthropist assisted her to rise, and he conducted her to another part of the room. Again the door of the court room was thrown open, and the busy officers led the way for a man and woman; the female bore in her arms a sleeping infant. She was wretchedly clad, but with a mother's tenderness she had wrapped her infant in a woolen shawl, and kept it close to her breast. The lazy spectators in the court room had witnessed so many scenes of wretchedness and misery that morning, as to have completely hardened their hearts to all feeling, and when these last prisoners took their seats in court, their abject misery furnished them with additional food for merriment. C. M., for it is he of whom we now speak, appeared like one whose measure of woe was full, and now indifferent to his fate. His dear wife had followed him, and now sat by his side, determined to share with him either for good or ill. Her frame appeared debilitated by long suffering, and her heart was full of anguish.

C—— M—— had been so often brought before the court for drunkenness, and been so often sentenced for such an offence, that his appearance did not cause any astonishment to the judge, the clerk, or the spectators and hangers on of the court room. His case had always been disposed of in a summary manner, and it was supposed that such a course would now be pursued, and little else did the poor inebriate, C—— M——, expect from the hands of the judge. And he was fully prepared for it, and felt not the pangs of insufferable woe which he had endured at other times, and he was prepared to meet his doom, for Hope, that sweet solace of all human trials, was nearly extinct within his breast.

But a new era in physical and moral reform had suddenly been commenced, and a bright and enduring page opened in the holy bond of humanity. For years, indeed, had man's ": inhumanity to man made countless millions to mourn," but now the inebriate was treated. as one suffering from an infirmity, and not guilty of a vice. The great moral enterprise of the Temperance reformation, led on by the noble champion *Hawkins*, was sweeping through the land, and under its influence, the errors and follies of the past were daily becoming vailed by the curtain of oblivion. It taught the great lesson, that even in the wretched and down-trodden drunkard there still lurks some moral excellence indicative of an immortal mind, and that where the power of the law was needed, it should be as a means of reformation, and not of vengeance. It taught the examples of our Saviour who forgave freely, not seven times, but seventy times seven. It taught the lessons of Him whose ways are infinite and unsearchable, who said " Him that cometh unto me, I will in no wise cast out." Among the signs of the times, all great distinctions were lost, the formidable barriers raised through false pride were broken down, and the noble work of charity unfettered by such distinctions, went forth free to perform its great mission. A ready hand of fellowship was extended to the inebriate, no matter how reduced in degradation, and he was assisted to rise out of the miry pit into which prejudice had cast him. And thousands found friends to sympathize with them, and when they formed the great resolution utterly and forever to forsake the infatuation of the tempter and destroyer, they were no longer suffered to linger behind in obscurity, but brought in front of the great curtain of life, to become active instruments in assisting their fellow sufferers to do likewise. And this noble work was not as formerly, viewed in the light of charity, but as a duty toward the suffering and unfortunate, who were brothers of the same human family. The great chord of the human heart was touched and a healthful tone imparted. This was to rouse once more a commendable pride, without which all labors of charity can be of little avail. The hand of friendship was extended toward the most degraded, and his heart so stimulated that he was prepared to go onward through dangers and difficulties which otherwise might confound and overwhelm him.

The great philanthropist to whom we have briefly alluded, is one of the most active disciples in the course of modern reformation; he is a Philanthropist, not in theory alone, but in practice. Toward the unfortunate his heart was full of pity, and all its kindliest feelings were exercised in alleviating their distresses. To the poor inebriate and that class of unfortunate females who had fallen victims to misplaced affection, and who were driven still deeper into despair by the harsh breath of slander, his sympathies were ever excited. He sought them in the lone hovel, and in those dark abodes where few had moral courage to approach, and then it was his pleasure to administer the sweets of consolation, to bind up the bruised heart when hope had fled. Few of the wealthy and prosperous of Boston know of the misery that dwells in their midst, or can conceive of the hours of tearful agony passed in secret by hundreds and thousands of virtuous and deserving beings, striving to recover from a load of misfortune, that threatens every moment to overwhelm them, and daily suffering in poverty with patience, and in secret with the hope that a better day was nigh. And such scenes as those which were hidden from the public eye, this devoted philanthropist sought, and in the midst of affliction, his active benevolence was abundantly rewarded. It was there that he held out inducements for reformation; it was there that he changed the clouds of sorrow to joy, and his influence like "a green oasis in the desert" again restored the rose to its wonted beauty, and changed an almost endless age of misfortune to a youthful and second spring of Hope.

When C—— M—— took the prisoner's stand to hear the charge read to him, his wretched appearance, rendered still more revolting from the effects of the delirium tremens, only called forth scoffing from the crowd of careless people, who could not find one extenuating circumstance in his favor, but were ready by their unfeeling conduct to crush him to death here, and send him unprepared to meet his God. But there was one present upon whose mind their cold and cruel animadversions had not the least effect, and that person was the kind-hearted philanthropist to whom we have briefly alluded. As this story is not one of fiction, but reality, and all the characters and incidents are from real life, we deem it proper in this connection, to give the name of JOHN AUGUSTUS as the gentleman who has so often been identified with acts of christian charity. He is a Philanthropist not in theory alone but in practice, and to his timely interference hundreds of innocent beings who have fallen under a variety of unforeseen circumstances, betrayed and lost, and hundreds more of the other sex, sunk deep in the dust by the hand of despair, have been won again, restored to new life, and are now bright lights in the world.

The philanthropist had this day done nobly, he had become bail for a number of forsaken persons, and every one present spoke in his praise, but the audience thought C—— M—— too far gone, ever to be redeemed, but "*Nil Desperandum*" was the motto of Mr. Augustus, and even in the lone and wretched M——, where others saw naught but matter for reviling, he discovered something that awakened the tear of sympathy; in that poor and almost broken and despairing heart he saw a precious jewel to be saved, in that cast off character, in that body which all else thought useless, he saw the immortal mind yet lingering, the vital spark had not fled, and he resolved to save it. The clerk finished reading the warrant and impatiently waited for the plea of the prisoner.

"Are you guilty or not guilty?" demanded he.

The prisoner raised his right hand trembling with delirium to his brow, as if to awaken a consciousness of his situation.

"There can be no doubt of his being a common drunkard," said the judge, "you see he is now suffering from the delirium tremens, but let us see what the witnesses have to say about him. The first witness may take the stand. Mr. Bat, what do you know about that man?"

Mr. Bat took the stand as was desired. "Please your Honor," commenced Mr. Bat obsequiously, "I've known him for two or three years, I think he's generally drunk; I guess I've seen him worse for liquor about ten times during two weeks, in fact I don't know as I ever saw him sober, he generally gets drunk in the morning and commences a new drunk before the old one is half over."

This remark of Mr. Bat's caused a loud laugh in the court.

"I don't know as it is necessary to go any further," said the judge. "The case is fully made out by Mr. Bat, and under that evidence I think it better to send him over. I suppose he has been to the House of Correction; does any officer in court know that fact?"

Two or three officers who were busily writing during this examination, dropped their pens from their mouths and stepped forward to answer the question of the court, but Mr. Bat being most interested in the result reached the stand first.

"I know, your Honor," replied Bat; "I know he has been there afore and I guess he's been there to speak within bounds at least a half a dozen times, and I guess I've committed him three or four times myself."

"Has he any family?" asked the judge.

"That is his wife and child," replied Bat, pointing to the half distracted Mrs. M——, who was standing by the side of her husband.

"They say she is a very clever sort of a lady and works hard to maintain her children, but he aint provided for them for a long time."

"For the best of all reasons, probably," said the philanthropist who stood near the prisoner. "He has been locked up in jail and in the House of Correction, he has been hunted by the laws and every infirmity of his nature punished. You have tried the experiment fully and now see before you a living witness of the folly of attempting to force a man into a reformation."

"I guess Mr. Augustus you'll find C—— M—— a hard nut to reform, and it's better for himself to go to the House of Correction," said Mr. Bat with some warmth.

"I think I can make a better use of him to keep him out of the House of Correction," replied Mr. Augustus.

The judge looked earnestly at the prisoner and conferred for a few minutes with the clerk.

"Do you think it worth while to give him a trial?" asked the judge of the philanthropist, "he appears to be a broken down man."

"I am willing to try," was his reply.

Two or three of the constables laughed at the idea of the philanthropist interfering with such a desperate case, and regarded him this time, like one of the Mr. Meddle school, who had entirely mistaken his place and was interfering with what did not at all concern him.

"Why, your Honor, he was drunk last night so he could not go," said one officer. "And the night before that, I saw him staggering through the streets," continued another. "And three days ago he was so drunk he could not walk straight, nor speak straight," said a third. "Why he gets as drunk as a beast, and I should as soon think of reforming a beast, I was going to say."

"Sometimes the most ferocious beasts are subdued by kindness and made as docile as lambs," calmly observed the philanthropist.

"I've talked to him, time and again, and given him a great deal of good advice, and told him no longer ago than day afore yesterday, if I saw him drunk again I'd commit him," said Bat with an air of consequence.

"And now I'll talk with him a little and do it I think in a different way from what you did," said the philanthropist, turning toward the prisoner. Mr. Augustus addressed his conversation in a low voice to the inebriate, and his wife; though his conversation could not be heard, it was very easy to see that his words had touched the heart of the prisoner.

The philanthropist wrote the name of the unfortunate man

upon a slip of paper, and arose for the purpose of addressing the judge; but the prisoner retained his hand in both of his, and pressed it to his lips, and when he lifted up his face, his eyes were filled with tears. The philanthropist had touched the right cord, and the divinity within, which had been smouldering in darkness for so many years, was again aroused, with all the feelings of manly pride. The hand of true friendship had been extended to him, and he grasped it with avidity. The clouds of despair that had hovered about his path, broke away, and the bright star of eternal hope again appeared before his bewildered eye. Amidst the storms and tempests of the past, "Hope enchanting smiles, and waves her golden hair;" and from the heart of the poor inebriate there gushed a fountain of tears: but they were tears of joy.

"What do you propose to do?" inquired the judge.

"I will be his bail for three weeks, from this day at eleven o'clock," replied Mr. Augustus; "and if at that time he is not an altered man, I will willingly consent to his becoming an inmate of the House of Correction."

"Very well," replied the judge; "you can take him—and I hope you may be successful."

Many of the selfish world might ridicule this act of the philanthropist in attempting to save one so degraded, and so long given over as incorrigible to all reformation, and perhaps would see little inducement for action in a being denounced by the world. But there is something nobler in the mind of the truly charitable than the gratification of the world's praise. If those to whom we refer could have seen those tearful eyes, and that look of joy, which had for the first time for so many long, long years, illuminated the face of the grateful wife of C—— M—— and could rightly have appreciated their feelings toward the philanthropist, they would have esteemed the enjoyment of that moment as a payment an hundred-fold for all the interest he had taken in their behalf."

To conclude this tale as briefly as possible, we may add that, by the continued efforts of myself,—by the blessing of

Heaven,—the subject of this sketch became a truly reformed man. The family have removed from the city, and are now comfortable and happy.

BRANDS FROM THE BURNING.

Twelve boys, all of about nine or ten years of age, were brought into the Boston Municipal Court one afternoon last week, to receive sentences for various criminal offences. They had been convicted, or had pleaded guilty, and their sentences had been standing postponed; some for nearly a year; others for less periods,—meanwhile they had been under bail. Most of them had been bailed by John Augustus. Their extreme youth, their circumstances, and the nature of their offences, caused the Court to grant this indulgence, in order to give an opportunity to secure their reformation, if possible, without farther interposition of the law. Mr. Augustus had been watching over them, procuring them employment, or securing their attendance at school; and as to each one, he testified that he could learn nothing against his honesty or good behavior during the term of his probation. With hardly an exception, they were very poor, some orphaned, generally bright-looking, and some of them very attractive in their appearance. Various certificates were read from their masters and employers. Court (Judge L. Cushing presiding) expressed great satisfaction at the good result which had so far followed the experiment made with these boys, and he delayed sentence further, in order that evidence might be adduced touching the ability of their friends to pay fines, which would reimburse the Commonwealth for the cost of prosecution. In those cases where such ability is wholly wanting, it was intimated that the sentences would probably be fines merely nominal.

It was a scene both affecting and encouraging. We congratulate the community upon the hopes thus entertained of rescuing those unfortunate children from the characters and careers of felons. We rejoice in the enlightened humanity of the Court; in the encouragement afforded to others to endeavor to save such children before they go far enough to reach the criminal bar; and we beg our readers to support and aid Mr. Augustus in his efforts.—*Christian World*, 1848.

POLICE DOINGS.

Before Justice Cushing. L. O., a girl of about sixteen, and who had been once before to the House of Correction, was charged with drunkenness, and plead guilty. When the arresting officer, on Saturday night, put her into the lock-up, she made an attempt to hang herself, but an alarm was made by another female prisoner, which brought the attention of the officer of the night, and he found her in nearly a strangled condition. He stated to the Court that, in his opinion, if she had been allowed two minutes more time, she would have accomplished the deed of suicide. The string was taken from her neck, and she was conveyed to the jail, where she declared that she was still determined to kill herself. The Court suspended sentence in the case, and gave John Augustus (who took an interest in her) leave to recognize for her appearance at this Court on the 12th of February. Augustus said he was not at all afraid that she would hang herself, and thought that, by the influence he could bring to bear on her, she would become a better girl.—*Daily Times*, 1850.

THE BEAUTIFUL CRIMINAL.

The young female, whose arraignment for drunkenness before the Police Court, we noticed some time since, and who was taken in charge by Mr. Augustus, has *not* since wandered from the path of rectitude, as was stated. Yesterday the period for which she was bailed, (on a trial of good behavior,) expired, and she appeared in court in charge of the "good philanthropist," who stated that she had been faithful and industrious; that she had resided with a family who desired not to part with her. She was fined one cent and costs, which

Mr. Augustus paid, and she left the court, looking an hundred per cent. better than when she was first brought up.

Her father died a drunkard's death, when she was but seven years of age. She lived then in Bangor, Me. After his death she was brought to Charlestown, where she entered the "street school," and learned to beg, lie, and pilfer. She followed that business until she was eleven. At fifteen she was the inmate of a house of prostitution. She was made so through the influence of a man now living in the State of Maine, and whose name is well known. She is but sixteen years old, and is now in good hands, and in a fair way of reformation.—*Bee.*

JOHN AUGUSTUS.

This noble philanthropist has in the kindest manner taken to his house Miss Ann W——, the lady who has been so villainously abused by John G——. It is exceedingly fortunate that in her desperate condition she has found so good a home. But for this she would have been thrown upon the cold charity of a too unfeeling public, and been again, perhaps, exposed to no less dangers than the one she has just incurred. He also provided for witness Julia B——, with cheer at his fireside. All honor to this truly practical philanthropist. They will both remain with him till the trial before the Municipal Court is concluded.—*Daily print*, 1850.

FRIENDS TO THE UNFORTUNATE.

There are classes of unfortunates in our city, and in all cities who find friends in a dark and evil hour; but we seldom hear of men whose benevolent labors extend to *all* cases where the least glimmer of hope in effecting a change for the better is noticed. There are two of these seldom-heard-of men in Boston, to our knowledge. We refer to John Augustus and John M. Spear, both of whom are constantly laboring to relieve distress. The theatre of their labor is in the courts, the prison, in lowly hovels, in garrets and cellars, in lanes and streets. There is room for others to labor in the same field.

A distinguished member of Congress, writing to Mr. Spear on the subject of his labor, closed with the following words of encouragement, which we are permitted to publish :—

* * * * * * *

"Your labors favor all classes; they tend to reform the prisoner; they render property more inviolable; they give additional security to every man's person, and every man's life; they make it less mournful to think of our common nature; and they help to remove one of the foulest stains from an age that aspires to be called Christian. You seem to me to be entitled to the aid and encouragement of all.

With my best hopes for your success, I remain very truly, your friend,   HORACE MANN.

West Newton, 1849."—*Bee*, 1850.

CRIME AND CRIMINALS.

There are many cases in which respectable security for the future good conduct of the offender, is sufficient to meet the full demand of justice. Now in these respects, the public magistrate of a large city, however merciful, cannot always trust his own clemency; for he represents the legal aspects of each individual case, and cannot often be acquainted with the circumstances which should mollify his decision. Hence the necessity of a prisoner's friend,—of one who shall assume the office of a Christian advocate, and shall represent the side of mercy in opposition to strict, untempered legality. We therefore regard the places filled by John Augustus and John M. Spear as essential to the full organization of our lower courts. Duties of this class might be reduced to legal form, and delegated to officers specially appointed for the purpose; but they are much more likely to be impartially discharged when they are the free-will offering of sincere philanthropy.— *Christian Register.*

DUTY OF SOCIETY TO THE PRISONER.

Extract from a Report.

Wendell Phillips' remarks were confined chiefly to the safety of society. In order to punish we must be able to appreciate and measure sin. Can man do this. No man *knows* what amount of good or evil exists in another heart. We have no right to approach a criminal to administer to him punishment, but rather to withhold him from doing more harm to others. Man has no right to punish. No man can commit crime without violating the laws of God. Man has no right to punish for such violation. God, who made his laws, let him avenge them.

"Punishment," says Lord Brougham, "however severe, does not deter criminals from committing crime." There is nothing more certain than that by proper treatment, the *first* may become the last offence. A large proportion of crime grows out of ignorance. More of the right kind of Education and proper treatment is demanded for the unfortunate classes of the community. By and by, the wisdom of the Legislature of this Commonwealth will become satisfied of these now unpopular truths, and will be glad to light its public torch at John Augustus' candle.

The thousands who crowd our shores from foreign lands, and who we have to take care of, are the ill results of the corrupted institutions of Europe, and should teach us important lessons in conducting the affairs of our own country. In answer to Carlyle's "Latter Day Pamphlet," on prisons, in which he describes the London prison as being so attractive in all its arrangements that the poor commit crime in order to become inmates of it, Mr. Phillips said, if the prisons of England are so good, then it speaks bad for the Christianity of that country, which keeps the outside so corrupt that people desire to get into prison. "I was in prison and ye visited me," is answer enough for Carlyle, said Mr. P.

THE PHILANTHROPIST FOILED.

Among the common drunkards sentenced to the House of
Correction by the Police Court yesterday, was a young Irish
girl named Sarah D——, who pleaded very earnestly to be
spared the misery of a confinement in the cells of convicts at
South Boston. This young woman was evidently not so far
gone in the dreadful vice as to put to flight a hope of a
thorough reformation, and Mr. John Augustus, the humane
gentleman whose good services and many noble acts of charity we have often recorded with pleasure, contemplated taking
her upon bail, which the law allows him to do, and placing
her as a domestic in his family, where he was confident she
would soon reform; but while he was making arrangements
out of court, the poor prisoner was hurried upon the stand,
examined, and doomed to the disgraceful punishment of a fel-
on, and which alone should be dealt out to crime, in the
House of Correction. She will come out in four months, from
this charnel-house of crime, a hundred times worse than when
she was turned in there. No drunkard ever has been or can
possibly be reformed by force, within the walls of a prison.—
Daily Mail, 1844.

FAMILY JARS.

E. W., a girl of sixteen years, was arraigned by her father, a
fierce looking relic of the late war in Greece, for assaulting
him and her mother. The mother and daughter are natives of
Athens, and are blessed not only with the peculiar features,
but the impulsive temper likewise, peculiar to the children of
that land of poverty and song. "Greece, but living Greece
no more." As it was a case of mere domestic amusement,
carried to unwonted excess, Mr. Augustus, with the consent
of all parties, undertook the settlement of the difficulty; but
in the end, he found it necessary to separate the girl and her
parents, until their hot blood should have time to cool; accordingly, she kissed her mother and the little ones, shook hands
with the father, and rode off with the peacemaker.—*Street-
er's Weekly Star*, 1846.

A RASCALLY SHAME.

A young girl not more than twelve years of age, pretty, intelligent and interesting, was complained of by a constable, as a drunkard, and a lewd and lascivious person. The incomparable officer would perhaps, have procured her conviction and imprisonment, but for the timely presence and interference of John Augustus, who defended her. She was discharged on payment of actual costs—*sixty-seven* cents. Mr. Augustus took the young creature to his own house where she will be properly cared for, and secured from the molestation of such men as this officer and his associates in vice and crime.—*Boston Herald*, 1848.

NEGLECT.

Margaret M. D., was seized with the cholera on Sunday morning, on the Mill dam, and allowed to remain uncared for in a suffering condition during the whole day until about seven o'clock in the evening, when John Augustus was sent for, who immediately conveyed the poor woman to the Hospital.—*Chronotype*, 1849.

[Extract of a Letter from Prof. F. Wayland.]

Providence, May 27, 1845.

* * * * * * Is it wise to have our annual reports so far *extempore?* What we sanction should be *ipsissima verba.* Our character as men is involved in what we hear, and order to be published.

2d. It seems to me that our expenditure should be used with great attention to results. The statistics which we have are important, but I doubt whether they always bear so closely on our object as they might. Why would it not be desirable to investigate the great subject of *pauperism*, and that of *criminal law*, which together, do almost the whole work of filling our prisons.

3d. Do the executive committee really take these subjects in hand, and give direction to the labors of the society? They have a very responsible situation and cannot discharge it by simply auditing bills. Can they not be induced to labor earnestly in this matter?

4th. It seems that JOHN AUGUSTUS, a poor man, has done much. We praise him. This is well. Can we not take means for following his example.

I am, my dear Sir, yours very truly,

F. WAYLAND.

CHAS. SUMNER, ESQ.

CRIMINAL STATISTICS OF BOSTON FOR 1846.

Of the men brought up as common drunkards, Mr. John Augustus bailed sixty-two. Four-fifths of them have done well, and two-thirds have paid the court costs. Of the women brought up for this offence, he bailed thirty-five, and of this number only five have relapsed.

The most interesting and pleasing achievements of Mr. Augustus have been, his interferences in favor of vagrant, pilfering boys. In three instances, he was perfectly successful. The boys were indicted in the Municipal Court for stealing. More wretched and abandoned looking objects were never described by Eugene Sue, yet Mr. Augustus undertook to save them. He went bail for them; had them cleaned and dressed up, and sent to school, and after keeping run of them for six months, he produced them in court perfect models of decent boys. Judge L. S. Cushing, satisfied that they had been reclaimed, allowed them to go without day and without trial.— *Daily Star,* 1847.

JOHN AUGUSTUS.

MY ESTEEMED FRIENDS. In passing by the place of business of that worthy philanthropist, John Augustus, I met that gentleman and was invited into his shop, to examine some documents relative to the noble work in which he is engaged; namely, in rescuing from the fangs of an unfeeling law, and restoring to life and usefulness, persons arraigned for crimes, mostly of a trivial character. These unfortunate persons, male and female, but for the timely influence of this genuine disciple of Jesus Christ, would receive the iron sentence of the law, and have to walk about like Cain, with the mark upon them, while the world would disregard that special protection granted by a merciful Father; and the law's last argument, the gallows, would most likely be the end of some of them.

John Augustus commenced the Christian work of being bail for offenders in 1841. The facts connected with his cause so finely, so beautifully illustrates the Omnipotence of the law of kindness, that it occurred to me to make a statement of them, knowing that your hearts beat responsive to those Christian principles, the carrying out of which has ensured these happy results.

For the first year Mr. Augustus did not include females in his efforts of relief, since that period very many of these have been rescued from a life of shame. His practice is (as you are aware,) to prevent the commitment to jail of accused persons, standing their bail, giving them counsel, assisting them to get employment, relieving their necessities, warning them of the woes their wicked course will bring upon them, and by kind and friendly treatment, winning them back to virtue, usefulness and the embrace of society. At times he has been under bonds to the amount of several thousand dollars, and is at this writing bound for over two thousand dollars, in sums of fifty to two hundred dollars; besides this he frequently advances money. The number of persons for whom he is now bound, is twenty-two, the whole number from the commencement, is over four hundred, he having preserved a list of their names, a bright shining list for the eye of the philanthropist.

Our friend Augustus appoints no committees, passes no resolutions, except in his own mind, has no presidents, vice presidents, secretaries, &c., but noiselessly goes right to work. Like his great MASTER, he literally "goes about doing good;" and doing much not included in the especial work now under notice.

In his labors he has visited the *very* worst haunts in the city, has taken the clenched fist of the infuriated moral maniac in his hands, and by the melting power of love, caused those fingers to relax their sanguinary grasp. He does not believe in bruising or killing men, either in war or singly, to make them happier or better.

But now comes the fact worthy to be remembered by every Christian and government on earth, throughout all coming time. Although the persons for whom Mr. Augustus has been bound were of course, not of the highest moral character, *yet only in one solitary instance*, has one of these forfeited the bail, and that person was a woman who did not appear from excessive fright. What was she afraid of? that this law of kindness would not continue to be exercised; thus proving its efficacy. Governments may here learn how much money they might save by the exercise of this policy; not to speak of the infinitely higher motives which should actuate them. The hawks that hover over and pluck out the eye of the dying lamb, cannot suddenly be expected to favor the removal of the wounded from the field of battle.

The course of this philanthropist, shows what might be done by an organized number of individuals, especially in visiting the sick, the afflicted, giving food, clothing, medicine, advice, encouragement, or whatever they had to spare. Suppose a society of this kind existed, districting the city, and by its committees, seeking out every object of distress, in poverty or crime, and affording such relief as they could, would it not be a Christian work? Suppose this Society should devote a portion of the Sabbath to this holy work, would it not be as acceptable to the Father of mercies, and more beneficial to man, than spending the same time in fixing the position of the altar, the point to which the face of the priest shall be directed when at prayer, or splitting hairs about doctrinal matters, the practical consequence of which, common sense has yet been unable to discover.

In the hope that the time may shortly come when criminals shall be treated as moral lunatics, and the whole family of man rejoice in the full fruition of the law of love,

I am sincerely your friend,
JAMES MITCHELL.

YOUTHFUL INTEMPERANCE.

In the Police Court this morning, a young and interesting
little girl, scarce twelve years of age, named Mary Ann G——,
was brought up by officer Eaton, charged with drunkenness.
She was found staggering about Ann street, and stated that
she obtained her liquor in the subterranean dens of that street,
which are a disgrace to the city. The mother of the little
girl died about a year since, and her father is absent with the
army in Mexico. She was delivered up to Mr. John Augustus,
upon the payment of a nominal fine of one cent and the actual
costs.—*Daily Evening Traveller,* 1847.

DRUNKENNESS,

And nothing else constituted the business of the Police
Court yesterday. Five specimens of common inebriation were
arraigned, three of whom were bailed by the working philanthropist, John Augustus—through whose efforts the most as-
tonishing results have been obtained, and reform induced in
the worst cases of vice as if by magic.—*Daily Mail,* 1845.

AN ODD FELLOW.

That genuine Independent Odd Fellow, JOHN AUGUSTUS,
was out on his daily mission of love and charity, at an early
hour in the morning of the great Odd Fellow's Celebration,
with his horse and carriage, traversing the city and seeking
out the real objects of benevolence, the poor, the suffering, the
down-trodden, in the obscure cellars and garrets, which are
seldom visited by any messenger from the busy world, except
himself. Mr. Augustus has invariably declined to connect
himself with any Lodge of Odd Fellows, whose principles he
so well illustrates in his life and labors. He is a Lodge in
himself—a true Odd Fellow, uncreated by any association or
body of men. The amount of good which he has done to the
unfortunate victims of intemperance especially, is almost incredible. He is the Howard of Boston.—*Mail,* 1845.

ANOTHER GIRL RESCUED.

At the house of Welch, the robber, spoken of in the Police report, officer Vialle found a little Irish girl, about 14 years of age, named Catharine G——, who had been taken a few weeks ago by Welch's wife, from a colored woman, keeping a brothel in the "black sea." This information officer V. communicated to Mr. Augustus, who sought her out, and took charge of her. Her story is, that about a month since, a lewd woman (now in the House of Correction,) coaxed her to run away from the Asylum in Providence, and placed her in the care of the colored hag, in the Black Sea; that while there, she was abused, because she would not submit to the contact of negro men, and that Mrs. Welch had taken her and treated her "ever so good." Mr. Augustus intends to send her back to Providence.—*Boston Daily Star*, 1846.

MR. JOHN AUGUSTUS.

MR. EDITOR: I saw an article in your paper of the 15th inst. which, by the way, I am almost ashamed to confess I do sometimes read, notwithstanding it is only fit for the mass, that led me to wonder at the state of things which admits of such conduct as was therein described, and still more of an allusion to it in terms of praise in a public print. It was headed "A Philanthropist," and went on to speak of one "John Augustus, a mechanic by occupation," as being actually engaged in works of benevolence, and actually saving money to the Commonwealth, by his judicious manner of standing up between the culprit and the offended majesty of the law, with his sooty hands as it were, pouring oil on the troubled waters that roll and rage, till their "ambitious head spits in the face of Heaven," in the vicinity of Court Street, Franklin Avenue, and Court Square. Now this is a little too bad : I find upon inquiry that it is all true. And that Augustus is not only a mechanic, but moreover a man of limited means. It is said that if he were called on for one tenth part only of the amount for which he is considered by the court

" good and sufficient surety," he could not muster it. Now
what a picture is this for the community to gaze at! Where
in the name of common sense is the necessity of schools, col-
leges, and *law schools*, if a man can have his workshop, it
may be a shoemaker's bench, and beard any young Lion of a
Counselor, with impunity in our very Court House; confront-
ing them as did a certain young carpenter years ago, by talk-
ing about kindness, mercy and love? Viri Romäe, Conic
Sections, classic Shades, Coke and Littleton, to say nothing of
Havana cigars and Back Creek oysters, has it come to this at
last?

This isn't all. Mr. Augustus not content with gaining his
point at law, must "enjoy the luxury of doing good" on *cred-
it*. This strikes at the root of every thing. State street must
now knock under, and the man who after a life spent in extor-
tion, hopes to make all right again by founding a hospital, or
endowing a charitable institution, sees with horror the smart
artisan begrimed with the dust of labor, doing away with the
possibility of these compromises with the Almighty, with as
much nonchalance as if he were driving a peg. This individual—no, this fellow, has also invaded the precincts of fashionable life. The Rodolphes, the Adrienne de Cardovilles,
the Angelina Wilhelmina Stubbses, will abandon their favorite
pastime. It is no longer distingué. French kid gloves and
Canton shawls,—let him reflect well on his course, who has
dared to drive these visitants from the dwellings of the poor!
Does he believe that one of those poor children of sorrow,
error, it may be of vice, whom he forsooth has led away from
her old haunts, to hold sweet converse with thoughts of better
days, would feel as willing to turn back to duty, in accordance
with suggestions from his week-day phiz, as if one of these
heavenly visitants bent over her like a faint embodiment of an
angel from above, striving to win her back to her father's fold
again? if so he is past help.

But the most dreadful part of this business is that Mr. Augustus goes to work on his own hook, and after his own fash-
on. To see him one would think it was his mission. H e

pays no respect to Sundays, does not think it important to wear a white neck cloth, nor is he even willing to confine his operations to any one parish or ward, but with the most complete verdancy " goes about doing good." Some shallow fanatics have said that this man's soul was cleaner than his apparel, but these are the " nigger men," who believe that the blacker a man is outside, the whiter he is inside. If this were the case, why wouldn't clergymen sometimes work? No, we need not disguise the fact. Mr. Augustus is undermining the foundations of church, as well as state. Every reformed inebriate, or returned prodigal, as in the quiet of midnight he kneels down in the little chamber of his father's house, where his early days of *innocence* were spent, and looks back on what but for a little timely aid he might have been, and forward to what by the help of God, he will yet be, and thinks gratefully of this mechanic, and calls down blessings on his head,—I say every such fellow is a vulgar wretch, not to have selected a more " respectable," not to say orthodox way of salvation. The idea—but there, the whole thing is too disgusting to go on with. What is to be done? I will suggest, though I do not want to take any part in the matter, on account of my family and advanced age, that some of the injured limbs of the law, a few of the clergy, and some whom I could name of my aristocratic friends, go in a body to Mr. Augustus's house after night-fall (he lives at 65 Chamber st.,) and throw some bottles of coal tar through his parlor windows. If that don't fix him, I don't know what will.

Yours very respectably connected,   M. A. O.

Chronotype, 1847.

THE LOST ONE FOUND.

The girl whose abduction we noticed in a paragraph yesterday forenoon, has been found. Mr. John Augustus discovered her yesterday afternoon in a certain house, which he declines to name, dressed in men's clothes, with hat and cane, and looking quite the gentleman. She was so neatly stuffed up to represent a youthful specimen of the opposite sex, that John Augustus had some difficulty in discovering the stray sheep in the disguise adopted. Measures have been taken to secure the option of a virtuous life to the girl who is barely 14 years of age —*Daily Times,* 1849.

The name of John Augustus is become familiar to the ears of the philanthropists of Boston and its vicinity. He is a boot and shoe maker, carrying on the business in Franklin Avenue, employing five or six men. In 1841, he first became interested in a man who was about to be sent to prison for the sin of rum drinking. Friend Augustus became bail for the inebriate, took him to his house, treated him kindly, induced him to sign the pledge, and made a good man of him. Since that time he has saved several hundred persons from prison, and from crime in the same way.

A Boston correspondent of the *New York Tribune,* thus speaks of a little incident which recently occurred, when he was in the shop of Mr. Augustus :—

"Having a desire to become acquainted with this remarkable man, and to get an old pair of boots rejuvenated, I stepped into his shop the other day, and while there an incident occurred, which will illustrate the almost reverential feeling entertained for him by those whom his kindness has saved from destruction. We were sitting in his counting-room, when an Irish woman whose appearance indicated that she had seen at least a fair share of the hardships of this world of ours, entered, made a courtesy, and with a deep brogue said:

'God bless your honor, I hope your honor isn't sick th'day ?"

The "man" informed her that his health was very good, and remarked that her countenance was very familiar to him, though he could not remember where he had met her before.

'It's very nathural,' she said, 'that you should forget the likes o' me ; but do you think I could forget your honor ?—

Wasn't it yersel' that paid the expinses of the coort, and saved me from the House o' Correction, where that spalpeen of an officer was goin' to take me off, and lave poor little Mike widout any mother to take care of him at all. An' didn't yer honor pay the wake's rent, when that could hearted landlord was goin' to sind me adhrift wid sorra a place to sleep in?—And wasn't it the kind things ye did, and the kind words ye spake to me that made a dacent, sober woman o' me, and kept me from taking a dhrop o' spirits from that day to this? And by God's blessing, I shall niver taste ardhent spirits again.—And isn't yersel' the cause o' all this? I shall invoke blessings on yer head, till the day o' my death, and tache the childer to do the same.'

There is no knowing how long the woman would have gone on showering her well deserved compliments upon her benefactor, had he not cut her story short by inquiring the object of her visit. She had come to see if Mr. A. could not obtain for her a pass or ticket of admission to the House of Correction, to her husband, or as she said, her 'ould man.'

Yours, ever,　　　　CLEVE.

IRRITABILITY AND COOLNESS.

The tedium of the Police Court is very often relieved by some slight passages at arms, between the clerk, Mr. Power, and John Augustus. The former carries rather the most weight, but the latter has the advantage in coolness, good nature and evenness of temper. Notwithstanding these little ebullitions, we have no doubt that the excellent clerk and phil-anthropic Augustus entertain the most sincere regard for each other.—*Herald*, 1842.

MR. AUGUSTUS.

We doubt not that some of the practitioners and officials in and about the Police Court, regard Mr. Augustus as rather a bore and hindrance to the despatch of business—perhaps as injurious to the profits of it. His action in a case may possibly diminish the number of lock-up fees. Professional cagers who look upon mankind as animals to be caged at so much a head, would be very likely on seeing the operations of Mr. Augustus to conceive a strong sympathy for the public, at seeing so many rogues turned loose on bail, among them.

The public, whose paid servants the courts, constables and jailors are, take a very different view of the matter; they view it very much as a man would who had twenty colts to break, and hired three or four jockeys to break them; they broke in and fairly tamed one, broke the neck of one, spent three weeks and a deal of money and flogging on the rest, and made them more untractable than they found them. Then came along an odd genius, who had a plan of his own for breaking colts, and just for fun, without asking a cent for it, coaxed down, tamed and made tolerable horses of three-fourths of the colts the jockeys had spoiled. With all due respect for judges, constables, courts and jails, and without presenting the cases as altogether parallel, we would suggest that the public has about the same feeling towards Mr. Augustus that the owner of the colts aforesaid, would have towards the volunteer colt breaker.—*Daily Chronotype,* 1847.

SAVED HIS FEE.

Mary Hill was complained of for drunkenness, by a Mr. Patten, of 17 Friend street, where Mrs. Hill with her husband boarded. Mr. Augustus became bail for her appearance on the 30th inst. for a further hearing. Meanwhile officer Stratton sent the woman out of the court room, thus depriving Mr. Augustus of his accustomed rule of looking after the parties whom he bails. Mr. Stratton arrested her, and found that by Mr. Augustus's benevolence, he was in danger of losing *seventy-five cents* in fees.—*Bee,* 1848.

JOHN AUGUSTUS.

Very few, probably, of the readers of the Rambler have not heard of John Augustus, the philanthropist. The history of his early charitable movements, has been given, and I will give only a few paragraphs relative to him at the present time. Personally, Mr. Augustus is a thin, elderly man, of medium height, his face somewhat wrinkled, and his features of a benevolent expression. Mr. Augustus is a warm-hearted and impulsive man. He generally utters what is uppermost in his thoughts, without stopping to calculate the effect which it will be likely to produce. This often gives to those who regard his operations with an envious or predjudiced eye, opportunity for a deal of fault-finding, which doubtless is quite gratifying to them,—a harmless amusement, as none who know the man would be in the slightest degree influenced by even the most bitter observations of his enemies.

In the Police Court, Mr. Augustus seems the most at home. As he enters the room, he casts his eye towards the prisoners' bench, where are seated perhaps, half a dozen miserable beings, bruised and ragged, and trembling from the effects of a recent debauch. It is probable that some of them know him, for as he walks to the box two or three turn their blood-shot eyes toward him with eager glances, endeavoring to attract his attention. In a moment he is with them, gently reproving the hardened ones, and cheering with words of encouragement those in whom are visible signs of penitence.

And there among the besotted and brutalized drunkards, sits a fair young girl. She has a studied look of defiance and apparent indifference, and the finery in which she is arrayed plainly indicates that she is one of the unfortunate class which modern fastidiousness forbids us to name, but which numbers its thousands in our city,—thousands drawn from every rank, and station in life. As the promiscuous crowd assembled in the room, gaze with curious and insulting stare upon the poor girl, she endeavors to assume a still bolder expression. Now Mr. Augustus approaches her, seats himself at her side, and converses with her in low tones. What he says you cannot hear, but you can very soon note the result. At first, she averts her head to prevent the crowd from noticing the look of shame which in spite of beauty, is showing itself in her face. And then you can see the feelings of sorrow, of contrition, exhibiting in her comely features. Presently her lips quiver, and soon she is violently and convulsively sobbing. Look at her now! Can you—*dare* you say that she is lost beyond the power of redemption?

The prisoners are arraigned, and the cases are severally disposed of. In some of them, Mr. Augustus sees that his interference would be of no use. In others, he becomes bail for the parties, who are set at liberty with the understanding that if they conduct themselves correctly, they will finally be leniently dealt with ; others have their fines paid ; and the philanthropist leaves the room, accompanied by the now humble and contrite pale one, who will be admitted into "the Home" where she will be surrounded with every influence favorable to reform.

As they pass through the door they are stopped by a wife, and mother, who pours out an avalanche of thanks and blessings on him, who has stepped in to save her loved, though erring husband.

Is not John Augustus a *happy* as well as a useful man? Believe he is!—*Rambler.*

PRACTICAL CHRISTIANITY.

In the Police Court, a woman named Martin, was brought up on a complaint for being a common drunkard, and Mr. John Augustus stepped up to move a continuance for three weeks. The officer who had had considerable trouble with her, rather demurred to the motion, and the judge asked him what kind of a woman she was. He replied, "she behaves very well when she is sober, but when she drinks she will rush into the street, take up a brickbat and send it through the first window she sees. That's the kind of a woman she is," said the officer. "No longer ago than yesterday Mr. Augustus undertook to talk with her and she spit in his face." Every body in court appeared astounded at this act of ingratitude, except Mr. Augustus, who meekly remarked, "Well, what of that; it didn't hurt me; besides, she was drunk then. Give me a chance to talk to her when she is sober and I'll answer for it, she won't spit in my face then." The court put the case off for a week and Mr. A. stood bail.—*Boston Post*, 1848.

POLICE COURT.

Mr. John Augustus, the well known philanthropist, appeared before the magistrate of the Police Court yesterday, and made favorable reports in the cases of several unfortunate victims of intemperance, &c., for whom he had been surety. Several had been completely reformed, and others were hopeful. Mr. Augustus has accomplished much good, and seems by no means weary in well doing.—*Boston Republican.*

GOOD TASTE.

* * * * Thomas Cox, the principal performer in the previous affray, was remanded until Wednesday, at eleven o'clock. Is it good taste for Mr. Augustus to shake hands with a man of this description, while under the charge of murder, and immediately after being arraigned? What should shaking hands mean?—*Daily Mail*, 1847.

OUTRAGEOUS.

Constable Jonas Stratton seized John Augustus, the philanthropist, yesterday forenoon, and attempted to thrust him by main force out of the court room, because there was no place where he could sit. This was done after Mr. Augustus had been told by another officer of the court that there had been no place assigned him, in the private stived up pens which have been *disarranged* for the lawyers and reporters. Such conduct ought not to be tolerated, nor would it be in a *justice* court room.—*Chronotype*, 1849.

MOCK PHILANTHROPIST.

There are a number of lazy, hypocritical knaves in the world who, by dint of unblushing impudence and affected kind-heartedness not only make a fat living by their mouthing professions, but actually pass with the credulous portion of mankind for real disinterested philanthropists. They may be found among societies of every possible name and description, and they collect large sums of money from all classes of the community ostensibly for some humane and charitable purpose, but in reality to fill their own coffers,—at least more than nine-tenths of all they beg and extort never reaches an inch nearer its legitimate destination. Slippery vagabonds who hate hard work, and doat on good living and a fat pocket book, readily and gladly abandon the lapstone, anvil or jack-plane to go on an easy and profitable mission of mercy.

We have known a goodly number of these sly, hollow-hearted charlatans and we never knew one of them who had a particle of honest disinterested love for any one but himself. We have been partly led into these remarks by the conduct of a fellow who is called John Augustus, by some, and by others, the "good Samaritan." This last epithet was applied to him in the first place, in sheer and sarcastic derision, by those who had sufficient penetration and knowledge of human nature, to see through his empty hypocrisy, and sufficient manliness to despise his audacious duplicity, and Augustus had it subsequently transferred in seeming earnest to some of our city newspapers, by a few threadbare chaps connected with the press, each of whom he rewarded with a pair of footed boots.

Mr. Augustus seems to have a great itching for notoriety, and dollars; at least, one would naturally think so, from the extraordinary pains which he takes to acquire both. He must have numberless modes of filling his purse, if one-tenth of all we have heard of him be true. Indeed, we have seen more than enough to satisfy ourself. He is overseer, or field-driver in a sort of Magdalen Asylum. The public will not need to be told any thing about the secrets of such establishments—

they have long since become proverbial. Under cover of this mysterious appointment, he hangs and loafs about the Police and Municipal Courts, almost every day, and takes more airs upon himself than all the judges and officers connected with both courts. His impudence has been increasing so rapidly that we had to rebuke him ourself, yesterday! We have been actually surprised at the license which has been given to this fellow, and Heaven knows we have never been a stickler for undue official rigor.

We have always been an inveterate detester of mock dignity, but we think it due to the character of a decent bar-room, that this Augustus should be kept a little more in his place. Who, we would ask, gave him a license to take uncontrolled possession of every woman that is brought up, or comes up to the Police and Municipal Courts? Are not the dignitaries of these establishments aware that while he is thus permitted to outrage the dignity of the court, that he is acquiring the means of bleeding thousands, and of gratifying his other propensities? They certainly cannot be foolish enough to suppose that he ever let an opportunity slip, of doing either. We know something about this Peter Funk philanthropist, and pea-nut reformer, and unless he conducts himself henceforth with a great deal more propriety, we shall take it upon ourself to teach him decency.—*Mike Walsh.*—Daily print, 1848.

FRIENDS TO THE UNFORTUNATE.

* * * * * * * What is more deserving censure than all the rest, is the unmanly flings at men who intercede for the victims of these avaricious men. God knows that if there is any person in the world that requires a friend, it is those poor, bold, debased, wretched, friendless girls who are brought into the Police Court. The great fear of John Augustus and John M. Spear on the part of the officers, is that they will diminish the business of the court.

That is the secret of all this complaint. There are those who undertake to say that John Augustus makes money out of the operation. Well, if he does we are glad of it. If a man can make money out of what we have known him to be about for the last few years, he deserves it. The best proof we have that John has not made money, however, is the fact that none of the persons who make such reports have gone into the business themselves. Men engaged in such business may sometimes be imprudent as they believe Mr. Augustus to be; but that don't justify sweeping assertions. We have rambled a little from our starting point, but have introduced nothing that does not naturally connect itself with the subject.—*Chronotype*, 1849.

POLICE COURT.—*Before Justice Cushing.*

Mary L—— was brought in for getting drunk, and found guilty. Mr. Augustus asked a little delay on the part of the court, in pronouncing the sentence, and set himself to work to bring about a reconciliation between the prisoner and her son-in-law, who had appeared in evidence against her, and who in the cross examination confessed that he was in the habit of carrying liquor into the house, and that his mother-in-law had opportunities to help herself as often as she pleased. Mr. Augustus succeeded in his purpose, and Mary returned to her home; Mr. A. becoming surety in the sum of $30, for her appearance on the 8th day of May. Mary promised abstinence for the future.

Elizabeth D—— was charged with drunkenness, and the charge was sustained by the testimony of two officers—who stated to the court that although the woman had twin children, two years old, at home, it would be an act of charity to send her to the House of Correction.

John Augustus wanted to know what would become of the children in that case and solicited the clemency of the court. The husband was present, and stated that while his wife was in the lock-up he had to take care of the babies; he too requested that his better half (although she had been a little the *worse* for liquor) might be permitted to return home on her promise not to "spree it" any more. The court ordered the payment of a fine of $2 and costs, total $7. Mr. A. again inquired "What will become of the children, your Honor?' "Why, Mr. Augustus," said the court, "you have done *your* duty and I have done mine." Elizabeth was taken away by the officers.—*Times*, 1849.

THE POLICE COURT ROOM.—ALTERATIONS.

This room has lately been undergoing alterations, and repairs. The reporter of the *Times*, speaking of the change, says, "No special compartment is set aside for the philanthropists—who are as useful a class as either the lawyers or reporters, although not holding legal recognition in court. As they inculcate the laws of charity and good will to men, they have no standing at the Massachusetts bar, and must therefore we suppose, fall back on the mercy of their co-laborers— the Reporters. For our part we say to Messrs. Spear and Augustus, welcome!"

We say *amen*, and second the welcome. It is too true, that "charity and good will to men," is seldom dispensed in the Police Court, except it be by the philanthropist or some one not officially connected with it.—*Chronotype.*

THE LAW OF KINDNESS.

A man by the name of M. N—— was returned to court by Mr. Augustus who had bailed him, on trial. The man said that he had not drank but once, and since then had taken the pledge. The judge gave him good advice, told him that during the short time which had been given him for trial he had done wrong to drink even once; and finally said that he would allow him three weeks more, for another trial. Mr. Augustus full of faith and hope that the man would do better, again became his security and Mr. N. left the court with his wife and beautiful daughter, who had been anxiously watching the result.—*Daily paper.*

HOW SOME THINGS ARE DONE.

On Wednesday in the Police Court, Mary D. the mother of four children, was complained of as a common drunkard. Mr. Augustus was about offering himself as bail for her when Mr. Stratton told him that if she was bailed, he would enter a complaint against her for an assault upon him, (Stratton), otherwise he would not. Mr. Augustus endeavored to persuade Stratton from such an unmanly course, but to no purpose. Then Mr. A. told the court that he would bail her nevertheless; accordingly he became surety for her.

Stratton immediately entered his new complaint and she was held to answer for an assault upon Mr. Stratton, "while in the performance of his duty." (If he handled her as we have seen him handle others, he did more than his duty and she or any one under the circumstances would be justified in resisting.) Mr. Augustus appeared as counsel for the woman. Stratton said the woman was turbulent and he threw or laid her down upon the floor and that while she was upon the floor, that she bit his leg. He was asked to show the pants, that the size of the wound might be known, *but the pants were at home!* He was then asked if he had any objection to show the wound, *and that he declined doing.*

Mr. Augustus then cross questioned the injured and to-be-pitied man, which made him appear in any thing but an enviable light. The judge then began to reprimand Mr. Augustus, for bailing the woman, and also scolded considerable because he seemed by his questions to doubt Stratton's word. Legal gentlemen in our hearing considered the questions of Mr. A. fair and just.

The woman was fined $10, and costs. Persons for assaulting officers are generally sent to the House of Correction. It must be gratifying to Mr. Stratton to know that the husband of this woman, who is a hard working man, will have to pay something like $15, before he can release his wife from Leverett street jail, where she has been sent just to gratify Stratton's spleen."—*Chronotype*, 1849.

CONCLUSION.

The preceding extracts have been given by request, and as this is my first, and probably the only report I shall ever issue, I have thought it advisable to comply with the request, and to publish a few of the many articles that have appeared in the public prints, both in favor and against my operations.

I have attempted to give a sketch of my labors, but the limits of the report preclude the possibility of my giving more than a very brief outline of them; I have inserted statistical tables in reference to cases that have come before the courts, in the period embraced in the report; these tables though concise, are strictly correct, and from them my friends will form a tolerably correct idea of the nature and extent of my labors in the courts.

I have a list of names comprising that of every man and woman sentenced for common, or simple drunkenness, within the last six years; to keep such a record may be comparatively an easy task, but it is quite a different matter to calculate the expense of punishing these offenders, for most of the items which make up the sum total of expense, have not been published, and are clouded in obscurity. No report upon these points is required, or expected from the keepers of any of the institutions; they are asked only, how many are committed for intemperance, how many have been addicted to intemperance, and other general questions. The records of Suffolk County Jail show a discrepancy in point of numbers, of three or four thousand drunkards, within a few years past, and gives no account of the expense of those they do report, which number consists only of those committed by order of the courts. Why should it not be known how many are discharged from jail, on the payment, or non-payment of fine and costs of court, as well as to know how many have been committed; and the question may be asked with equal propriety in reference to the House of Correction. At present we can know nothing of the number of those who are discharged on payment of fine and costs, or those who are discharged without such payment.

In 1850 there were 137 persons who were ordered to stand committed to the House of Correction for non-payment of fines and costs, and more or less are sent over for the same cause every year; but it appears from another report, or Pauper's Abstract, that all these, are regarded as *paupers*. Now to send so many able bodied men and women to this institution for drunkenness, and then to report them as paupers, and as nothing is reported from which we can learn whether they have been and are an expense or not, is a policy the utility of which I cannot understand. The temperance lecturers tell us that temperate drinkers pass through different stages of inebriety, till at last they become paupers, but it now appears that a shorter way is discovered, for if a person is proven to have been intoxicated three times within six months preceding the date of the complaint, he is called a common drunkard, and is at once sentenced to Deer Island, or, in other words, the Poor House, for a period assigned by the discretion of the court.

In this manner, during the last year three hundred persons were sentenced there from the Police Court, as common drunkards, and of this number one hundred—fifty-one males and forty-nine females—were committed in the months of July and August.

During the month of July last, fifty men were sentenced as common drunkards, at the Police Court; twenty-nine of this number were sentenced to the House of Industry, having a number of months allotted them to labor, equal to one man's work for seven years and four months. It was a very busy season of the year, and by far the greater number of these men were strong and well able to labor, and no doubt earned more than their living. The same month, forty-five women were sentenced in the same manner; thirty of this number were sent to the same place, having a period allotted them for work, equal to the labor of one woman for nine years, and most of these women were able to labor. Thus it appears that during one month a sufficient number of persons were sentenced to this institution, to perform an amount of labor, which it would require *sixteen years* for one person to do. During the years 1850 and 1851, five hundred and thirty persons were thus sentenced, but notwithstanding this vast amount of labor, no other report is made of them than that they help to swell the number of paupers of Suffolk County, the record of which is sent to the Secretary's office.

It may appear from my tables, that all cases of intemperance reported from the House of Correction, were of common drunkards, but the fact is, quite a number have been committed there for non-payment of fine and costs. Of the 137 that were ordered to stand committed in 1850, it does not appear how many paid their fines and costs, before or after commitment, or whether they ever paid them. In view of these facts it appears that there is a deficiency in the requirements of information upon those points.

I will mention one or two instances in which paupers are made so, from being sentenced for a period of time to Deer Island, or to the House of Correction. Families are thus broken up,—parents sentenced as common drunkards and the helpless children, of course, becoming at once a public charge. I may also mention an instance when the sentence of a fine of $2, and costs, has made paupers.

There was a family who lived in Spring street, and who consisted of a mother and six children. The mother was addicted to intemperance, and was at length carried before the Police Court, and sentenced to Deer Island. The children were left without any one to take care of them, and they were all therefore, permitted to go to the Alms-house. After the expiration of the term of imprisonment of the mother, she was discharged and returned to her former abode, but her furniture, scanty though it were, had been stolen, thrown away or otherwise disposed of, and the house was occupied by another family, who were strangers to her; she had no home,—it was a wet day, her shoes were thin and torn, and her clothing was insufficient to protect her from the inclemency of the weather. She sank down, disheartened and discouraged, and wept bitterly; her children for whom she still felt a mother's affection, were left behind. In a fit of despair she entered a rum shop and tasted the first glass, with a view to drown her troubles. This course she pursued until she was again arrested and sentenced to the House of Correction; she went there more degraded than when she went to the Island. What finally became of this miserable family, I do not know. Could she have had a friend at first to have bailed her, in all probability, she and her children would have been saved from this kind of pauperism.

There occurred another, and a similar case in South street. The family consisted of a mother and three children. Her landlord was a grocer and rum seller, and she lived in a chamber over his shop. When she moved there she was a decent, hard-working woman, but drank occasionally, she however, took proper care of her family. She purchased her provisions of this man, and no material change was observed in her conduct, for five months after she moved there, but it was evident that she had during this time, given more indulgence to her appetite for intoxicating liquor. She finally became unable to take care of her children, and neglected herself sadly; she became too destitute to procure means to pay for a loaf of bread for her children, but by some means managed to obtain rum, till at length she was taken to the Police Court, and sentenced to the House of Correction, for three months.

When the officers started to convey her over, they drove the carriage to the woman's abode to take her children to the Poor House, and the little ones, unconscious of the degradation, regarded it as a great indulgence to be permitted to ride with their mother. I was there when the carriage drove up in front of the rum shop, and I helped the children into it; the mother was crying; one of the little girls fell down into the mud and was considerably hurt, but it only caused a laugh from the landlord who stood near by.

In tones of mock sympathy, he told the woman that he was sorry to see her going off in that way, and said if she had listened to his advice she would have been better off. She reproached him with being the cause of her trouble, as he had sold her liquor, and as the carriage moved off, she uttered a curse upon him which called forth a loud laugh from the brutal landlord. Thus was a whole family made paupers at once.

I knew a poor woman in Endicott street to sell half a barrel of flour, which she had purchased by hard labor, for her own use, for half its value, to a grocer, to obtain money to pay her husband's fine and the costs of court, incident upon his examination. It amounted to five dollars, and before she could raise the amount, and go to the Court House, her husband had been sent to the House of Correction. Still in hope of saving him, she hastened to South Boston, but when she got there, to her surprise and grief, she learned that the bill had grown larger, and her scanty sum which she had raised was insufficient to pay it, and with an aching heart, she was obliged to return to her destitute home and leave him. How long he remained there I do not know.

The next case that I will mention, is that of a woman who lived in East Boston; and who was addicted to the use of intoxicating liquor. She had a sick child, over whom she watched anxiously, and with a fond mother's affection ; for two or three successive nights she alone watched by its cradle, and on the fourth it died; it was buried the next day. The day following she labored as hard as usual,—for the poor must work in their grief—and in the evening, was tempted to drink ; she got intoxicated, and at an early hour was arrested by an officer, and taken to court; there she was found guilty and sentenced to pay a fine of two dollars and costs, and for want of this sum was committed to jail. It was the first time she was ever arrested. I visited her in jail; she appeared well and expressed the deepest regret for her conduct ; she wept bitterly as she told me her sad story. She had just lost a child, another had been carried to the Poor House. She was in jail for an indefinite time, and the court, she said, had refused to hear her story. Her cup of misery was full.

There was no need of putting this woman in jail. In old times, if people were dealt with in this manner, scarcely a clergyman would have been safe, and most certainly the deacons would have been "sent over."

This case is one of the four thousand three hundred of which I have spoken, and was just such a one as have for the last six years been disposed of in the Police Court, by a sentence of a fine of two dollars and costs. Of the four thousand three hundred, three hundred and fifty within the last six years, were ordered to be committed to the House of Correction, till the fines and costs were paid. Here is a great difficulty, and a matter which appears to demand legislative action: the clerk of the Police Court makes his report that he has received certain sums of money, but no one knows for what; nothing is said upon this point.

Why should not the people know how much it costs to reform drunkards, when it costs the city so much to make them so? There is the same want of definiteness in the jailor's report and in that of the House of Correction.

On March 28, 1846, a man named R. A., was sentenced to pay a fine of three dollars, or to be imprisoned two months in the House of Correction; and that year, a girl was committed at the same place for non-payment of fine and costs. She went there, I think, in July, and her friends knew nothing of her whereabouts. One day a gentlemen called on me, and said that his wife wished to find this girl, but thought from what she had heard, that she was in the House of Correction, and requested me to ascertain if such was the fact. I called upon Justice Merrill, of the Police Court, and at my request he examined the records of the court, but her name could not be found, as there had been no report of her; the next day we made further search, and learned that she was in the House of Correction, but would soon be discharged, as she had been there nearly three months, and they could only keep her till the expiration of that time. I accordingly went to this gentleman's house and informed him how she was situated, and advised his wife to let her stay there two or three weeks longer, and she would then be discharged without payment of the fine and costs, for which she was imprisoned; but to this she objected, and giving me the money to pay the fine, requested me to procure her immediate discharge. The next day I called at the office of the overseers to obtain a permit to visit the House of Correction to effect her release. Dr. Moriarty was present. I told him what I desired; he was loath to give me the permit, but after asking me several questions he gave me one. It read as follows :

"City Hall, Office of the Overseers of the House of Correction.

Tuesday, Oct. 13*th,* 1846.
To the MASTER OF THE HOUSE OF CORRECTION.

Sir,—Please admit Mr. John Augustus to see Mary Timiney, if in his opinion practicable.

J. MORIARTY, *Overseer.*"

With this permit I went to South Boston to effect my purpose. I was well aware that the overseer did not appreciate my labors, but on the contrary, regarded me as a meddler in other people's matters, and probably said of me, as did Mr. Power, Clerk of the Police Court, "that I was always meddling with other people's business." I went to the gate and presented my permit to Mr. Faxon, the gate-keeper; but he replied that he was sorry that he could not admit me. I asked him the reason for the denial; he said he did not know, but such were his orders. I showed him my permit, and pointed to the overseer's signature; but he said argument was useless,—he must obey his orders, and I was obliged to come back without being admitted.

I reported the result of my visit. The gentleman advised me to call upon Mayor Davis the next morning, and obtain a permit from him. But the authorities at the House of Correction probably anticipated some action on my part, and on the opening of the Police Court, the next morning, Justice Merrill informed me that the woman had been discharged. A report had been hurried over early that morning; but how a quorum of Justices had so speedily been assembled, I was at a loss to understand.

The following instance will also illustrate the difficulty of obtaining the discharge of a prisoner from Jail or from the House of Correction, when imprisoned for non-payment of fine and costs.

On the 24th of January, 1850, a man by the name of Edward Hunt was brought before the Police Court and fined two dollars and costs for simple drunkenness, and was ordered to stand committed to the House of Correction till paid. He was very poor, and being unable to pay the fine, was committed. Up to the 20th of February, there had been no report at the Police Court of this man being in the House of Correction; but after some difficulty, we ascertained that he was there. He—like most drinking men—had a good wife; she had two bright, intelligent boys, the older being six years of age. He was taken sick with the small-pox on the 23d of the month, and died on the 25th. I was called to see her. It was early in the evening that I entered the house. The body of the child lay in a corner of the little room; the heart-broken mother sat upon a low box, having the other child, very sick with the disease, in her lap. The mother wept bitterly. There was no light in the room, and the poor creature had no money to procure any. Another destitute woman, who lived in the house, was making every effort in her power to comfort the mourner. My heart ached for her as I inquired what I should do. I procured a light, and gave her a sum of money to purchase a few necessary articles till further provision could be made for her. She had not tasted a morsel of food that day, and had she desired it, it was not in the house. I offered her food, but she said, "No, Mr. Augustus; I want you to get Edward out of the House of Correction, that he may see James before he is buried. If you will, I know the Lord will bless you." I promised her I would, thinking, of course, that there could be no doubt of my success under such circumstances. The next morning I went to the Police Court. Justice Merrill was officiating for Justice Cushing, he being absent. I related all the circumstances of the case, and requested the discharge of the man. He very indifferently replied, that he was only there

for a short time, while Mr. Cushing was absent; and Mr.
Rogers was ill at his boarding-house,—and therefore nothing
could be done. I told him the case was an extraordinary one,
and no man with a spark of humanity could find fault if he
should order his discharge. I pressed him so hard upon this
point that he became impatient, as I thought. I labored that
forenoon to accomplish the object. I ascertained where Justice Rogers boarded, and went to his house. He was confined
to his room by illness, but was able to see me.

I related the story to him, and told him also of the com-
munication I had had with Justice Merrill; and Judge Rogers
wrote the following note to Mr. Cushing:—

"Judge Cushing :

Dear Sir,—I will take notice of any
meeting, and you and Judge Merrill may do any thing which
you see fit. I do not go out to-day. It seems that sickness
and death might be an exception to our rule.

Yours truly,   J. G. Rogers."

I carried the note to Mr. Merrill, but he said he could not
discharge him because Justice Cushing was absent; and I was
finally disappointed, notwithstanding the note of Mr. Rogers.
I was compelled to carry the sad intelligence to the mother,
who wept bitterly, as she knew that the body of her child
must be buried under such circumstances. I could, perhaps,
imagine her feelings. It appeared as if the Justices of the
Police Court could not trust each other to do a good act alone.
Justice Merrill had refused on the ground that their rules
required two, or all three of them to be present, before any
thing of this kind could be performed. One would quite
naturally suppose that they might place confidence in each
other, at least sufficient to give such an order in such extreme
cases. But we hope that ere long this requirement may be
amended.

Another duty devolves upon the Justices of the Police Court,
which is to discharge all those who are confined in jail, or in

the House of Correction, for non-payment of fines and costs. By the established rules, the Jailer and the Master of the House of Correction are required to present a list or report of all those who are committed for non-payment of fines and costs, and who are unable to pay. It is also a rule of the Justices to have such reports brought in on the first and third Wednesday of each month. This is an arrangement which, though evidently made to save time, and as a matter of personal convenience to themselves, appears to be very objectionable; for at such times, both the Police and the Justice's Courts are in session, and no one can tell what part of the day the report will be taken up, as it depends wholly upon the amount of business before them. Hence the relatives and friends of those reported, are prevented from being heard when they wish to state the condition and circumstances of the parties. I have sometimes known persons to wait all the forenoon, and be finally compelled to return home without knowing whether those in whose behalf they wished to speak were discharged or not.

Again, the manner in which this report is examined by them, appears also objectionable; as it is, no one other than themselves can understand it. The Justices all may be very humane, and intend to do well, but established rules of this kind have a tendency to harden their sensibilities. Sometimes this hasty examination is proceeded with, and those persons are not discharged who would have been, had the Justices heard and believed the statements of the friends of such persons, in their behalf. Why should not this docket or report be called in a similar manner to the docket of the upper courts, at certain times, and allow the parties interested an opportunity to make their statements concerning such persons? Many of the rules of the Police Court are oppressive, and should be either amended, or give place to others of a more salutary kind. In this court, if a person be sentenced to three or four months imprisonment in the House of Correction, even if the most weighty mitigating circumstances of the offence be afterwards stated, it is of no use, the sentence has been uttered—the decree has gone forth out of the mouth of the Justice and cannot be changed. I never knew a sentence of this kind withdrawn to afford an opportunity to bail the person, yet occasionally the sentence is somewhat reduced. Happily, such a state of things does not exist in the Municipal Court; here there is not half that oppression that there is in the Police Court, and we hope the time is not far distant when all oppressive rules in that court; whether originating with the Whigs, Democrats, or Free-soilers, will be ruled out of court.

All the judges of the Court of Common Pleas seem to be men possessed with a large share of benevolence; they are always willing and careful to hear all mitigating circumstances before sentence; and after sentence, if there should any thing appear which would have modified it, the matter receives their immediate attention and careful action. Their organs of *caution* are just prominent enough to hold back on *benevolence*, so as to result in impartial justice, mingled with mercy, and when they close the term for which they preside, righteousness and peace follow in their footsteps.

The judges of the Court of Common Pleas should have the discretionary power of discharging those persons who are confined in jail for non-payment of fine and costs, when sentenced, without the necessity of aid from the Police Justices. As the law exists at present, a person in jail for such a cause, may petition the Justices of the Police Court for a discharge, after first having obtained the consent of the judge who sentenced him, and getting the signature of this judge to a petition to that effect; an assemblage of Justices of the Police Court may then be obtained, and after all this ceremony, if the Justices consent, he is finally discharged. Why should not the judge who sentenced the person have the power to discharge him, in an urgent case, instead of the waste of time and trouble spent in convening two or three Justices? During the time spent in this manner, the person whom we were aiming to relieve might die. This law must and will eventually be changed, and we hope that time is not far distant. The following case forcibly illustrates the necessity of a change in this respect.

A woman named Josephine Gallatin, was committed to the lock-up, for an assault; she there took poison and was then sent to jail, from which she was, by order of Dr. Clark, sent to the Hospital; afterwards, on the statement of the physician there, that she was able to be removed, she was recommitted to jail, when it appeared that two blood vessels had been ruptured, and her health was in a precarious condition. Mr. Andrews, the jailer, very humanely endeavored to effect her removal from jail, but Judge Rogers said that she could not, by the law be removed, unless she was bailed; no one came forward for that purpose but myself, and I was required to go through an examination in regard to competency, which I could not do, and in a day or two afterward, the woman was found dead in her cell. In this case, Mr. Andrews exerted himself to the extent of his ability to obtain her discharge, but to no purpose; and I may here say, that Mr. Andrews was one of the best men to act as a Deputy Jailer that ever filled the office; he was ever ready to assist those whom he could consistently aid, and to attend upon the calls of the sick. I have more than once known him to take money from his own pocket to purchase articles for their comfort. One night, a woman who was there for non-payment of fine and costs, was taken violently ill late in the evening; Dr. Clark was called, and said she must be immediately removed from the jail. The fine and costs amounted to fifteen dollars, and there was no way to discharge her till this amount was paid, other than by the long process above mentioned; her husband was utterly unable to pay even a part of this sum, and Mr. Andrews very kindly offered to pay one-half of it himself; several of us paid the balance, and in an hour afterward the woman was removed to her home.

It would perhaps, appear incredible, and the limits of this work will not allow of multiplying melancholy and painful instances to show how much good might be done for the relief of suffering in this way, should suitable persons enter this field of labor. At present, Mr. J. M. Spear is engaged heart and hand in this good work; he visits the jail very frequently, and therefore, well knows the wants of certain prisoners, and also knows that there are very many there who are deserving of assistance, and more that might be saved than he and I both can attend to. My report has far exceeded in size the limit I first designed, yet I cannot close without saying a few words more.

In August, 1850, as I was walking around in Leveret street jail, I found a small boy who was crying. I asked him why he was there, and he said he did not know. I inquired of the officers and they informed me that he was there on charge of committing a rape; at first, I paid no attention to the reply, thinking of course, that the statement was false, but I afterwards learned, that such was the fact. He was but *seven* years old. I proceeded directly to court, and informed his Honor, Judge Hoar, who was then presiding, of the fact. The judge immediately issued a *capias* and the child was brought into court. By advice, he pleaded not guilty. A jury was impanneled in the case, and though the presumption was that the judge's instruction to the jury would result in the boy's acquittal, just as the trial was about to proceed, I told the judge that I thought it a shame and a disgrace to all present to proceed with the case; his Honor asked what could be done; I replied, "let him be sent to his mother and placed in her lap;" I stated that I would bail him, and to this the court readily assented. I bailed him, then moved to have the indictment placed on file, which was done, and I carried the child to his home in Chelsea. This is the only case where I became bail when the indictment was laid on file on a plea of not guilty, except perhaps, when parties have died. The Grand Jury were not aware that the charge which they investigated was against so young a child. The girl upon whom the assault was alleged to have been committed was but ten years old.

I have bailed persons charged with all sorts of crimes bailable on the Statute book, but only now and then a case like the above. Some people will insist that I do more harm than good in bailing so many. They say it is of no use to complain of boys or girls, or women, for I manage to get them discharged; that all sorts of crimes, even rape and highway robbery, may be committed with impunity, and I will bail them. But this representation is false. I have indeed bailed a party charged with the crime of rape, and also in a case cf highway robbery, and as I have related the former, I will briefly give the other.

Sometime during the year 1847, two boys were at play on the Tremont road, and finally got to quarreling; one seized the other's cap, and the other in return took six cents from the first; they then separated. Soon after, the first returned with the cap, and claimed the six cents, but the boy who had taken the money was not disposed to give it up, and a prosecution at the Police Court was the consequence of the refusal. The boy was arrested on a charge of committing highway robbery, and was confined in jail. His father applied to me to bail him, and I did so; afterwards the parents of the boys, by consent of the court, settled the matter satisfactorily to themselves; and here ended the great highway robbery case. One of the boys was nine, and the other ten years old. In former times a birch rod would have been law and gospel to them both.

I have endeavored to give an idea of my labor for the last few years of my life. For my own gratification I have caused the name of nearly every person whom I have bailed, to be placed on a docket or roll, which, at the present time measures *sixteen yards* in length. It contains the names of eleven hundred persons, both male and female, and only one of them has ever forfeited the bonds; if only one-half of this number have become reformed, I have ample cause to be satisfied.

In the Municipal table is a number of persons who were indicted for all offences bailable by law; of this number one hundred and sixteen were boys under sixeeen years of age; eighty-seven ·were under the age of fourteen; twenty-seven were under twelve years, and four were only seven years old. Of this number only twelve were incorrigible, and were sentenced by the court; one was sentenced to the State Prison for crimes committed while under bail; five were sent to the State Reform School, and six to the House of Juvenile Offenders, at South Boston. I have always endeavored to send these persons to school, or some place of employment, and but *two*, to my knowledge, have stolen since I bailed them, and this shows that nine out of ten have behaved well; but had only half of them done well, the result would have been truly encouraging. The cases of some of them whom I bailed last fall, have not yet been disposed of; and I am happy to add, that these persons are doing well. I have given the number of persons brought before the Police Court for drunkenness, for the last six years, but I presume that if the number of persons were known who have in this time, been arrested by the watch for this offence, and subsequently discharged without being taken to court, the whole number would have been double what it now appears. Many of those arrested by the watch have been conducted home to their families, and others have been discharged in the morning, by the kindness of the captain of the watch.

I have made every possible effort to reform the drunkard, and have been called to visit hundreds of families where some person was drunk, which cases were distinct from those at the courts. The calls of this kind were quite sufficient to have occupied all my time that I could spare. In many of these cases the parties were respectable, having both character and money, and yet stood in need of a friendly adviser, by whose timely aid much cost as well as disgrace and unhappiness has been prevented.

' The race is not always to the swift.' The acorn is the germ of the mighty oak, and the performance of an act small in itself, may be attended with consequences too great to be calculated. The following instance illustrates this principle.

One evening in the year 1845, I was in Commercial street, when about twenty emigrants who had arrived in Train's ship, entered a room for temporary shelter. This group and the place, formed a picture of wretchedness, which transferred to canvass, would awaken emotions of sympathy and pity. There were no chairs in the room, and the miserable objects were seated on the floor. One girl in particular, arrested my attention. She was apparently about fifteen years old, a countenance prepossessing, an intelligent eye, and in her general appearance, far from being displeasing or repulsive, as many of her companions actually were; she was crying, and my curiosity and an interest in her welfare, led me to make some inquiries into her history. She had no home or friends; her mother had died on the passage, and she was left penniless in a land of strangers. I took her to my house where she remained for a week or two. A lady from Roxbury took her into her family as a domestic, and she proved to be a very good girl. The lady who was very kind, took especial pains to instruct her properly in her duties, and she remained in this family until the spring of 1851, when she was married to a very respectable man in Watertown, who had acquired a snug little property of about seven thousand dollars, and a happier pair cannot be found.

Before closing this report I would impress upon the temperance societies the necessity of more vigorous action. There have been lectures upon this great reform movement, but at present as in the past, there seems to be a want of more practical labor in our city. By practical labor in this field, I wish to be understood, that the friends of temperance should visit the abode of the drunkard, and by direct contact with him endeavor to improve his condition and restore him to his sphere in society, by the removal of unfavorable influences. If the friends of the inebriate wish to accomplish his reform, let them visit our Police Court, and by conversation with him they are shown all the avenues of vice by which he is surrounded; they learn where he lives, become acquainted with the condition of his family, and can more effectually apply their efforts for his welfare by bailing him.

I wish my brethren of the Sons of Temperance would more frequently visit the families of drunkards, for by so doing they would be the better prepared to administer that aid, advice and solace that is required, and the suggestion will be equally applicable to all other temperance societies of whatever name.

In this sketch of my labors I have endeavored to avoid the mention of any thing which might give offence; I have purposely omitted the mention of much that has tended to cramp my efforts, or to wound my feelings, and I have no doubt that the labors in this field for those who may hereafter enter upon the work, will be much lighter and far more agreeable. Within a few years past the spirit of reform and improvement has pervaded our city institutions, and many desirable changes have been wrought. Ten years ago there was no such thing as speaking to a prisoner in jail, now I am allowed to converse with them; humanity is now a qualification of a jailer. In the Municipal Court room, within the last two or three years, I have felt that I was not regarded as an intruder, all the officers, the sheriff, the county attorney, and the reporters for the daily papers, the clerk and the crier, have all been friendly to my labors, and have often rendered me great assistance, and all have my sincere thanks. The judges unanimously, have expressed their approval of my object and labors in court. The clouds which at first were dark and threatening, have been dispelled.

There is however, much opposition to the plan of bailing on probation. Those who are opposed to this method, tell us that it is rather an incentive to crime, and therefore, instead of proving salutary, it is detrimental to the interest of society, and so far from having a tendency to reform the persons bailed, it rather presents inducements for them to continue a career of crime; the law is robbed of its terrors, and its punishments, and there is nothing therefore, to deter them from repeating the offence with which they were previously charged.

The premises upon which such reasoning is based is incorrect. Individuals and communities generally are but too prone to infer evil of a class, if they but occasionally observe it in individuals; if a person who has been bailed, or received the leniency of the court, proves false to his promises of amendment, people are ever ready to predict that all others will conduct in a similar manner; and this they persist in believing, although instances are very frequent, even three to one, where such persons have become good citizens, and regain their former station and relation in society. I shall leave the matter for others to discuss and decide, but I am content, feeling as I do, that by such humane means hundreds of the fallen have been raised even by my humble instrumentality.

I shall not probably, for another ten years, should I live, attempt to work in this manner on so large a scale as I have done, yet this conclusion is not the result of any change of opinion respecting its efficacy. My age and my general health will doubtless prevent in a measure, my usefulness in this department of labor, and I most sincerely hope that some person will come forth and enter upon the work. I hope also, that Mr. Spear will continue his labors and prosper abundantly, and be well supported in his labors of saving the fallen.

As I have spoken somewhat at length upon matters relating to my work in Suffolk county in aid of prisoners, and more particularly of drunkards, it may not be uninteresting to my friends to know something in reference to the extent of intemperance in the various counties of the Commonwealth, as I have worked more or less in several of them.

There has been committed to the different Houses of Correction in the State, within the last six years, sixteen thousand and seventy criminals for various offences; of this number, eight thousand, four hundred and eighteen were committed for drunkenness. By the returns, it appears there has been committed to the different jails, eight thousand for the same offence, of this number all but two hundred are confined to five counties; but no one can exactly tell of what this number is a part, for as I have already said, it is quite difficult to ascertain the amount of expense for the punishment, or as some say, the reform of the drunkard.

It has cost forty thousand dollars merely to commit these prisoners to the jails, leaving out of the calculation all the expense that has followed.

I have given some facts in reference to the House of Correction of Suffolk, and might also of several other counties; it has cost Middlesex county, the last six years, twenty-five thousand dollars as their share, to reform drunkards. Bristol county has paid in the same time, forty-three thousand dollars for the support of two thousand five hundred and forty-nine criminals, and of this number one thousand seven hundred and sixty-two were drunkards, so that the number committed for other offences is but six hundred and seventy-one. Should not the county commissioners be required to investigate the matter at the jails, as well as the Houses of Correction, that the public may obtain more information than they now do upon these points?

The following table shows the increase and decrease of drunkenness for the last six years, in each county. We have several times applied to the Legislature for the establishment of an asylum for inebriates. We desire something different from a House of Correction or Alms-house, in order to save an honest man from being thrust into a den of thieves and robbers, where they are compelled to work side by side; we desire also, a place where he may be able to earn something for the support of his family. The present mode of disposing of this unfortunate class of criminals is faulty and defective. They are sentenced to the House of Correction, where they can earn nothing for their families; and often just as they begin to make some proficiency in a particular branch of business their term of imprisonment expires, and they are discharged. If they could have been sentenced for a longer period, and their families could have derived some benefit from their labor, it would have been for their own welfare, and in very many cases, would save their wives and children from the Alms-house.

It is extremely desirable that an asylum of the character to which I have briefly alluded, should be established, in six of the counties of the State,—especially is this desirable if the increase of drunkards for six years to come is likely to prove as large as it has for the six years past.

Those who may not be familiar with the criminal calendar of the State will doubtless feel interested in an examination of the following table.

TABLE,

SHOWING THE COMMITMENTS IN THE STATE, &c.

COUNTIES.	SUFFOLK.		ESSEX.		MIDDLESEX.		WORCESTER.		NORFOLK.		HAMPDEN.		BRISTOL.	
TIME.	Whole Number.	Drunkenness.	Whole Number.	Drunkenness.	Whole Number.	Drunkenness.	Whole Number.	Drunkenness.	Whole Number.	Drunkenness.	Whole Number.	Drunkenness.	Whole Number.	Drunkenness.
1846	857	518	123	69	443	245	117	58	57	33	95	46	281	210
1847	823	428	158	78	369	165	160	58	60	34	78	42	363	267
1848	933	471	137	85	398	212	241	80	85	52	121	65	439	283
1849	1164	502	255	140	444	255	256	96	92	58	161	95	482	354
1850	1085	460	355	205	424	212	283	160	92	46	298	158	479	317
1851	1132	454	350	191	503	264	283	126	105	50	197	98	506	381
Total,	5094	2833	1378	768	2581	1353	1339	578	491	273	950	504	2549	1762

COUNTIES.	FRANKLIN.		BERKSHIRE.		PLYMOUTH.		HAMPSHIRE.		BARNSTABLE.		NANTUCKET.		DUKES.	
TIME.	Whole Number.	Drunkenness.	Whole Number.	Drunkenness.	Whole Number.	Drunkenness.	Whole Number.	Drunkenness.	Whole Number.	Drunkenness.	Whole Number.	Drunkenness.	Whole Number.	Drunkenness.
1846	12	3	39	3	19	14	13	9	6	0	0	0	0	0
1847	11	9	37	10	18	4	3	1	8	0	2	0	2	0
1848	21	11	60	19	15	10	no return	0	no return	0	7	6	2	0
1849	12	5	94	50	20	14	29	16	10	5	16	14	0	0
1850	16	8	70	26	23	13	55	27	10	1	7	6	2	1
1851	12	7	77	28	26	11	22	11	10	2	8	7	3	2
Total,	84	43	377	136	121	66	122	64	44	8	40	33	9	3

I shall continue my labors as heretofore, provided the recently appointed county attorney, sheriff and jailer should coincide with my plans, and I have no doubt they will, and thus there will be a concert of action agreeable to all, the judges having unanimously expressed their approval of my labors. Those whom I have bailed, nine out of ten have been very poor, and unable to employ counsel; nine out of ten of them who were guilty have by my advice, pleaded guilty, and thus saved the Commonwealth the expense of a trial in each case. Of the eleven hundred whom I have bailed, in no case was it understood that I was to receive any remuneration for so doing; and of this number there were only ten who ever gave me even a cent; in the case of these the act was wholly voluntary; hence it appears that not one in a hundred have ever paid me any thing. Those persons were bailed at the Municipal Court, and in that court I have paid for others more than five times the amount of the sum given by those ten persons. During the period embraced in this report I have bailed over five hundred persons as common drunkards, in the Police Court, who, after the expiration of the period of probation, were sentenced to pay a fine of one cent and costs, the amount of which will be seen by reference to the Police table; and of this sum I have paid six hundred dollars, nor did I ever receive a dollar from any of them. I have been very particular upon this point, as there are persons who believe, or affect to believe that I make money by such acts; while it saves the county and State hundreds, and I may say, thousands of dollars, it drains my pockets, instead of enriching me. To attempt to make money by bailing poor people would prove an impossibility.

The first year and the three or four years following, I worked hard at my business in my shop. Sometimes I worked all night to make up for the time I had spent in court. I was obliged to prepare work for my workmen, and thus my duties were extremely laborious. I expended all I earned for four years, by hard labor at my trade, besides what aid I received from others. The first two years, 1841–2, I received nothing from any one except what I earned by my daily labor; in

1843, I received from various persons in aid of my work, seven hundred and fifty-eight dollars; in 1844-5-6, I received twelve hundred and thirteen dollars each year. I then gave up business at my shop, and for the last five years, my receipts have averaged, yearly, seventeen hundred and seventy-six dollars, all of which I have expended, and have not a dollar of this sum. The money which I have thus received came from kind friends to the cause in which I was engaged. I have the names of these persons, but do not feel at liberty to give publicity to them, as they are not of that class who wish "to stand at the corners of the streets to be seen of men."

I have kept an account for the last six years, of the amount I have expended, and for what purposes it has been applied. If I had had more, I should have expended more, for I have not had enough to render my labors so easy or so efficient as they would have been, had I more money.

The scenes which I have described have fallen under my own observation, and what remarks I have made, upon any of the institutions or officers, have been made, not in a spirit of fault-finding, but with a view of offering some suggestions for improvement. Others may differ from me in their views upon these subjects, and have of course, the right to express their opinion,—the liberty of speech being guaranteed to all. But if I have inadvertently misrepresented any thing I shall at any time be ready to make all necessary corrections.

If any one who is professedly expert in book-making should discover a multiplicity of errors in my style of writing and mode of expression, let my apology be, that my time has not been spent in getting out *books*, but in getting *persons* out of jail. If there are any who wish to render me assistance by pecuniary aid or otherwise, or any who desire information or assistance which I can render, in my field of labor, I should be happy to see them at my residence, No. 65 Chamber street.

It will, I trust, afford peculiar satisfaction to those who have aided me to know, that the funds which they have contributed have not been misapplied.

I respectfully submit this sketch of my labors, to my friends and the public.   JOHN AUGUSTUS.

INDEX

INDEX

* new material added

PATTERSON SMITH REPRINT SERIES IN
CRIMINOLOGY, LAW ENFORCEMENT, AND SOCIAL PROBLEMS

* new material added   † new edition, revised or enlarged

* new material added † new edition, revised or enlarged